Revise WJEC

GCSE English and English Literature

Barry Childs

Ken Elliott

Margaret Graham

Ted Snell

www.heinemann.co.uk
✓ Free online support
✓ Useful weblinks
✓ 24 hour online ordering

01865 888080

Heinemann is an imprint of Pearson Education Limited, a company incorporated in England and Wales, having its registered office at Edinburgh Gate, Harlow, Essex, CM20 2JE. Registered company number: 872828

www.heinemann.co.uk

Heinemann is a registered trademark of Pearson Education Ltd

Text © Pearson Education Limited, 2009

First published 2009

13 12 11 10 09
10 9 8 7 6 5 4 3 2

British Library Cataloguing in Publication Data is available from

ISBN 978 0 435368 11 1

Designed by Tony Richardson (Wooden Ark, Leeds)
Typeset by TechType, Abingdon
Cover design by Tony Richardson (Wooden Ark, Leeds)
Picture research by Maria Joannou
Printed in China (CTPS/02)

Acknowledgements
The author and publisher would like to thank the following individuals and organisations for permission to reproduce photographs:

p5 ©Photolibrary/Fancy/Beau Lark; p8 ©Corbis/Will & Deni McIntyre; p11 ©The Anthony Blake Photo Library/Alamy; p13 ©Corbis/Hugo Philpott/EPA; p16 ©Photodisc; p21 ©Dan Guravich/CORBIS; p23 Harry Taylor/Dorling Kindersley; p25 ©luxxtek/iStockphoto; p29 ©nick free/iStockphoto; p31 ©Getty Images; p33 ©Getty Images/Stone; p35 ©Dave Hogan/Getty Images; p38 ©Cathrine Wessel/CORBIS; p45 (Bill Bryson) ©Rex Features/Geoff Moore; p45 (Trail sign) ©David James Harris; p48 ©Photolibrary/Mauritius/Pepperprint pepperprint; p50 ©aldra/iStockphoto; pp52, 64 ©Getty Images/Hulton Archive/Val Doone; p54 ©Ted Horowitz/CORBIS; p55 ©Getty Images/Hulton Archive; p57 ©Getty Images/Michael Steele; p73 ©Corbis/Helen Atkinson/Reuters; p74 ©London Aerial Photo Library/CORBIS; p75 ©Corbis/Mike Segar/Reuters; p80 ©Getty Images/Taxi; p85 ©Photolibrary/Banana Stock; p89 ©LUCASFILM/PARAMOUNT PICTURES/THE KOBAL COLLECTION; p90 ©Alamy Images/dbimages/Jeremy Graham; p92 ©Picture Desk/Kobal Collection/United Artists; p97 ©Getty Images; p100 ©Getty Images/Color Day Production; p103 ©Topham Picturepoint/Elliott Franks/ArenaPAL; p105 ©Topham Picturepoint/Roger-Viollet; p107 NORRINGTON Nigel/ArenaPAL/TopFoto; p109 ©Chris Jackson/Getty Images; p113 ©Corbis/Robert Llewellyn; p114 ©Shutterstock; p116 ©Getty Images/FPG/Hulton Archive.

Every effort has been made to contact copyright holders of material reproduced in this book. Any omissions will be rectified in subsequent printings if notice is given to the publishers.

Extracts from *Man and Boy* by Tony Parsons. © 1999 Tony Parsons. Used with permission from Harper Collins Publishers; Extracts from short story 'The End of the World' by Arthur C. Clarke. © Arthur C. Clarke. From *Story – an anthology of stories and pictures*, published by Penguin. Permission granted by David Higham Associates; Extracts from short story 'Help' by Penelope Lively. © Penelope Lively. From *Pack of Cards*, published by Penguin. Permission granted by David Higham Associates; Extract from short story 'Clap Hands, here comes Charlie' by Beryl Bainbridge. © Beryl Bainbridge. From *Mum and Mrs Armitage*, published by Duckworth, 1985. Used with permission from Johnson and Alcock; Extracts from *Tears of the Giraffe* by Alexander McCall Smith are reproduced by permission of Polygon, an imprint of Birlinn Ltd. www.birlinn.co.uk; Book cover image of *Tears of the Giraffe* used by kind permission of Little Brown Book Group; Extracts from 'A Piece of Wood' by Ray Bradbury. Reprinted with kind permission of Don Congdon Associates; Extract from short story 'Hannah'. From *Have the Men Had Enough?* by Margaret Forster, published by Chatto & Windus. Reprinted by permission of the Random House Group Ltd; Extract from *A Walk in the Woods* by Bill Bryson, published by Doubleday. Reprinted by permission of the Random House Group Ltd; Extracts from the Captive Animals website are used with kind permission of the Captive Animals' Protection Society. www.captiveanimals.org; Extracts from *The Road to Wigan Pier* by George Orwell (Copyright © George Orwell, 1937). Reprinted by permission of Bill Hamilton as the Literary Executor of the Estate of the Late Sonia Brownell Orwell and Secker & Warburg ltd; Extract from *Notes from a Small Island* by Bill Bryson, published by Doubleday. Reprinted by permission of the Random House Group Ltd; The Blackpool Zoo leaflet has been used with kind permission of the Blackpool Zoo; Leaflet from Sheffield used by kind permission of the Leisure Tourism Manager for Yorkshire South Tourism; Poem 'A London Thoroughfare 2AM' by Amy Lowell; Poem 'Stars and Planets', from *The Poems of Normal MacCaig* by Norman MacCaig. Reproduced by permission of Polygon, an imprint of Birlinn Ltd. www.birlinn.co.uk; Poem 'Autumn' by Alan Bold is used with the kind permission of Alice Bold; Poem 'Woman Work' by Maya Angelou, from *Still I Rise* © 1986 Maya Angelou. Published by Little Brown. Used with permission.

Extracts used in the CD-ROM: Extract from *To Kill a Mockingbird* Copyright © Harper Lee, by kind permission of Aitken Alexander Associates Ltd; Extract from *Of Mice and Men* by John Steinbeck, published by Penguin Books; Extract from *Blood Brothers* © 1985 by Willy Russell. Used with kind permission of Casarotto Ramsay; Extract from *A View from the Bridge* by Arthur Miller. © 1955, Arthur Miller. Reproduced by permission. All rights reserved.

Contents

How will this book help me?

This book will take you through the types of questions that you will face in the exams, whether you are taking Foundation Tier or Higher Tier. You will also find examples of exam answers written by students to help improve your responses. The examiners then give their comments on these sample answers together with advice on how they could have been improved. Then it is your turn to have a go at sample exam questions. These are provided to help you revise actively and prepare for your real exams.

On the CD-ROM you will find additional student answers, guidance and extracts. The CD-ROM icon indicates where there is content in the CD-ROM.

What is in the GCSE English Literature exam?

There is one exam paper in English Literature, whether you are taking Foundation Tier or Higher Tier.

How long is the exam?	Two and a half hours
What is in the exam?	Section A contains questions on your set novel. Section B contains questions on your set play. Section C requires you to write a response on a poem you probably have not seen before (the 'unseen poem').
What is in Section A?	Part (a) contains a printed extract from your set novel, and a question (or two questions, in the Foundation tier) on this extract. Part (a) is worth 10 marks. Part (b) requires you to write an essay based on your set novel. You are given a choice of two essays. This essay is worth 20 marks.
How much should be written?	Depending on handwriting size, you should aim to write at least a side to a side and a half for the extract question, and about three sides for the essay question.
How long should be spent on Section A?	You should spend about 20 minutes on the extract and 40 minutes on the essay (an hour in total).
What is in Section B?	Part (a) contains a printed extract from your set play, and a question (or two questions, in the Foundation tier) on this extract. Part (a) is worth 10 marks. Part (b) requires you to write an essay based on your set play. You are given a choice of two essays. This essay is worth 20 marks.
How much should be written?	Depending on handwriting size, you should aim to write at least a side to a side and a half for the extract question, and about three sides for the essay question.
How long should be spent on Section B?	You should spend about 20 minutes on the extract and 40 minutes on the essay (an hour in total).
What is in Section C?	In this section, a poem is printed and you are asked to write about it, giving your response.
How much should be written?	Between one and two sides, depending on handwriting size.
How long should be spent on Section C?	You should spend about 30 minutes, including reading and thinking, as well as writing.

What is in the GCSE English exams?

There are two exam papers in GCSE English, whether you are taking Foundation Tier or Higher Tier. These are as follows.

	Paper 1	Paper 2
How long is the exam?	2 hours	2 hours
What is in the exam?	Section A is a test of Reading. Section B is a test of Writing.	Section A is a test of Reading. Section B is a test of Writing.
What is in Section A?	There is a short story or extract from a novel of about one-and-a-half sides in length followed by four questions each carrying 10 marks. On the Foundation Tier, occasionally, there will be two questions worth 5 marks and three worth 10 marks each.	There are two passages to read – one a media text and the other non-fiction. There will be four questions on the texts each carrying 10 marks. One of the questions will ask to compare the texts in some way. On the Foundation Tier, occasionally, there will be two questions worth 5 marks and three worth 10 marks each.
How much should be written?	Depending on handwriting size, you should aim to write between two-thirds and a side for each answer in Section A.	Depending on handwriting size, you should aim to write about half to one side for each answer in Section A (except for those requiring a list!).
How long should be spent on Section A?	About 55 minutes	About 50 minutes (no more than 1 hour)
What is in Section B?	Students will be asked to produce two pieces of writing. Each is worth 20 marks.	Students will be asked to produce two pieces of writing. Each is worth 20 marks.
What are the tasks?	There is one task that requires students to inform/explain/describe – with the emphasis on the last of these (i.e. description). The second task, from five choices, requires students to explore/imagine/entertain (i.e. personal experience or story).	There is one task that requires students to argue/persuade/advise. There is another task that requires students to analyse/review/comment.
How much should be written?	Task 1: Depending on handwriting size, you should aim to write about one side. Task 2: Depending on handwriting size, you should aim to write about two sides.	Depending on handwriting size, you should aim to write between one and two sides for each piece of writing.
How long should be spent on Section B?	About 65 minutes: 25 minutes on the first task and 40 minutes on the second task.	About 70 minutes, so about 35 minutes on each piece of writing (no less than 30 minutes).

Reading

Paper 1 Section A at a glance

The reading section in Paper 1 will contain a story or part of a story and usually you will be asked to tackle four questions. Each of these is worth 10 marks, though sometimes there are three 10-mark questions and two 5-mark questions. There are five main types of questions, and practising each type will increase your confidence when you sit the examination. The five types of questions are:

Type 1: Locating and retrieving information

- What clues or details can you find to prove something?
- What evidence can you find to prove something?

Type 2: Personal response

- What are your thoughts and feelings about a character or relationship or place?
- What impressions do you get of a character or relationship or place?
- What do you learn about a character or relationship or place?

Type 3: Character response

- What are the character's thoughts and feelings?
- What is going through the character's mind?
- How does a character react or behave or change?
- Why does a character act or behave in a certain way?

Type 4: The craft of the writer

- How does the writer convey, create, make or suggest such things as excitement or tension or drama in this section of the story?
- What happens in these lines? How and why do you react to what happens?
- How effective is the ending?
- What are your thoughts and feelings as you read these lines?

Type 5: Empathetic response

- Imagine you are a character. Write about the incident/events in the passage from your point of view.

Locating and retrieving information

Key revision points

- Reading the text line by line is really important – the examination paper will sometimes remind you to 'track the text'. Often the points you are looking for may come quickly one after another, even in quite short passages of text.
- The questions will usually refer to specific lines of the text. So the instructions will often tell you to 'Read again lines xx to xx'. Make absolutely certain that your answer is based on **just** those lines. It's a good idea to mark each section of text on the examination paper. Anything you say from outside these lines will not earn you any marks.
- Make sure that each point or comment you make is clear and makes sense. It is often useful to support your comments with a short quotation from the passage.
- The mark allocation (in brackets) gives you a guide as to the time you should spend on the answer. A 10-mark question should take you no more than about 13 minutes, but try to make sure your answer covers all the lines you are directed to look at. Questions are usually worth 10 marks, although occasionally you will find 5-mark questions.

Sample 5-mark question and answer

Read the passage below, taken from a past exam paper, then read the sample student answer and the examiner's comments that follow.

The kindly headmistress came and led us into the assembly hall. She gave us a brief, breezy pep talk and then the children were all assigned to their
5 individual classrooms.

Pat got Miss Waterhouse, and with a handful of other parents and new kids we were marched off to her class by one of the trusted older children who were
10 acting as guides. Our guide was a boy of around eight years old. Pat stared up at him, dumbstruck with admiration.

In Miss Waterhouse's class a flock of five-year-olds were sitting cross-legged on the floor, patiently waiting for a story from their teacher, a
15 young woman with the hysterical good humour of a game-show host.

'Welcome, everyone!' Miss Waterhouse said. 'You're just in time for our morning story. But first it's time for everyone to say goodbye to their mummy.' She beamed at me. 'And daddy.'

It was time to leave him.

From *Man and Boy* by Tony Parsons

Sample question

What details suggest this is a school where parents were happy to send their children? **(5)**

Sample answer

> Parents would like to send their children to this school because the headmistress was a kind lady who led all of the parents to the assembly hall. She gave them some brief news about what class the new children are going to. Some of the children in the school are so kind that they volunteered to guide the parents of the new schoolchildren. Miss Waterhouse was a kind teacher who read stories to the children. When the parents come in with their children, all the class patiently wait for their teacher to come and read them a story.

Examiner's comments

This answer would get a reasonable mark, although it needs to identify more of the details that suggest why parents are happy to send their children here. It over-uses the word 'kind', and a stronger answer would make more use of the words in the passage to collect marks. The answer makes a reasonable point about the headmistress, sees that the children are both helpful and well-behaved and attempts a comment about Miss Waterhouse. This would achieve a D grade.

How to improve this answer

- The point about the headmistress being 'kindly' would get a mark. However, the passage also tells us that she gave a 'brief, breezy pep talk'; this suggests that she is efficient, informative and reassuring to parents. So, the sample answer could make more of the second sentence.
- The 'pupil guides' also suggest good organisation as well as well-behaved pupils who can be trusted; again, this is rather more than just being 'kind'.
- The pupils' good behaviour is mentioned again as they wait 'patiently' for Miss Waterhouse. It also suggests they enjoy the stories that the teacher reads to them.

- Miss Waterhouse welcomes the parents as well as the children and is described as having 'good humour', again something parents would welcome. You would gain marks for the point about welcoming everybody and about her good humour. The student's comment on her is just a little limited.
- To move the sample answer from a D grade to a C grade, it would simply need to include one or two of the additional details mentioned here.

Tips

- Track through each sentence, making sure you miss nothing about Harry.
- Remember that even a single word can be selected to prove the point you wish to make.

Your turn!

Now it's your turn to show you can read carefully, and select appropriate details. Read the extract below and answer the question before it. The extract is from the same novel and here the father, Harry, a single parent, is taking his son, Pat, to the school for the first time.

Harry is clearly feeling uncomfortable as he arrives at the school. What details from the passage make this clear? **(5)**

◀◀ Timing

As a rough guide, you should spend no more than about 13–14 minutes to write an answer to a 10-mark question. If you are given a 5-mark question, as you are here, don't spend longer than about 6–7 minutes on it.

As we drove closer to the school I was seized by a moment of panic. There were children everywhere, swarms of them all in exactly the same clothes as Pat, all heading in the same direction as us. I could lose him in here. I could lose him forever.

5 We pulled up some way from the school gates. There were cars double-parked and treble-parked everywhere. Tiny girls with Leonardo DiCaprio lunch boxes scrambled out of off-road vehicles the size of Panzer tanks. Bigger boys with Arsenal and Manchester United kitbags climbed out of old bangers. The noise from this three-foot-high tribe

10 was unbelievable.

I took Pat's clammy hand and we joined the throng. I could see a collection of small, bewildered new kids and their nervous parents milling about in the playground [...]

A lot of the children starting school had both parents with them.

15 But I wasn't the only lone parent. I wasn't even the only man.

There was another solo father, maybe ten years older than me, a worn out business type accompanying a composed little girl with a rucksack bearing the grinning mugs of some boy band I had never heard of. We exchanged a quick look and then he avoided my eyes, as

20 if what I had might be catching. I suppose his wife could have been at work. I suppose she could have been anywhere.

From *Man and Boy* by Tony Parsons

 Sample 10-mark question and answer

Read the passage below, then look at the sample student answer and the examiner's comments on the answer. Remember that for a 10-mark question, you should aim to write your answer in about 13–14 minutes.

The thick furs thudded softly to the ground as Professor Millward jerked himself upright on the narrow bed. This time, he was sure, it had been no dream:
5   the freezing air that rasped against his lungs still seemed to echo with the sound that had come crashing out of the night [...]

All was quiet again [...] The world was
10   utterly still: even in the old days the city would have been silent on such a night, and it was doubly silent now.

Professor Millward shuffled out of bed, and [...] made his way slowly
15   towards the nearest window, pausing now and then to rest his hand lovingly on the volumes he had guarded all these years.

He shielded his eyes from the brilliant moonlight and peered out into the night. The sky was cloudless: the sound he had heard had
20   not been thunder, whatever it might have been. It had come from the north, and, even as he waited, it came again [...]

Only Man, he was sure, could have made such a sound. Perhaps the dream that had kept him here [...] for more than twenty years would soon be a dream no longer. Men were returning to England, blasting
25   their way through the ice and snow with the weapons which science had given them before the coming of the Dust [...]

The broken sea of snow-covered roofs lay bathed in the bitter moonlight. Miles away the tall stacks of Battersea Power Station glimmered like thin white ghosts beneath the night sky. Now that the
30   dome of St Paul's had collapsed beneath the weight of snow, they alone challenged his supremacy [...] Twenty years ago he had watched the last helicopters climbing heavily out of Regent's Park, their rotors churning the ceaselessly falling snow. Even then, when the silence had closed around him, he could not bring himself to believe that the
35   north had been abandoned forever. Yet already he had waited a whole generation, among the books to which he dedicated his life.

From 'The End of the World' by Arthur C. Clarke

Sample question

The setting of the story is London in the future. What evidence is there in these lines that it is in a future very different from now? **(10)**

Sample answer

The first thing that suggests it is in a future very different from now is when it says, 'Men were returning to England.' This suggests that for some reason everyone had left England which is obviously very different to how it is today ✓. 'Through the ice and snow'. London is not often covered with ice and snow so this is very different to how it is today.

'He had watched the last helicopters climbing heavily out.' This suggests it must be in the future because helicopters weren't around 20 years ago. Again it suggests that everyone is leaving.

'Ceaselessly falling snow'. If it snows in London it will stop after a few days; by saying 'ceaselessly' it shows that the snow won't stop falling which is very different ✓.

'England has been abandoned forever.' This has never happened before so it shows it must be in the future ✓.

'St Paul's had collapsed'. This building is still in use today so, as it has collapsed, it must be a different future ✓.

This is not tracked methodically. Notice how far down the text this quote is taken from.

No reward – this quote doesn't emphasise the continual ice and snow in this future.

No reward – this is simply wrong.

This is just repeating the point already rewarded.

Examiner's comments

This improves towards the end, after a very shaky opening. The opening half of the passage has been ignored and this makes it difficult to gain a high mark. When the student finds some evidence and makes an appropriate comment, the marks are gained. However, there are just not enough details mentioned to gain a C grade and, as it stands, this answer would be awarded a D grade.

How to improve this answer

Always track the text from the very beginning of the passage. In the very first sentence, we learn that Professor Millward is using 'thick furs'. This and the freezing conditions suggest climate change and the suggestion is clear that it is in an ice age. It is also clear that London is silent, 'The world was utterly still' and as we read the passage, we learn that London is now deserted, apart from Professor Millward. We learn he is guarding books ('volumes'), again suggesting that the world is a very different place from the London we would know. Throughout the passage, there are lots of details that reinforce the key points about London being deserted and being covered in snow and ice for a very long time.

Your turn!

Now it's your turn to show you can read carefully, and select appropriate details. Read the extract below and answer the question before it.

What evidence is there in the passage that Jenny struggles to cope with running the house?   (10)

Henry said, 'You'll have to get some help.' He said it in the quiet, level tone that meant there was to be no discussion, the matter was decided now. But none the less Jenny said, 'What?' She said it not because she had not heard, but, like

5   a child, because she did not want to hear.

'You'll have to get some help. I'm tired of this mess.'

Guiltily, Jenny followed his glance across the smeared table [...] the children's coats tumbled behind the sofa, the clutter of toys and newspapers in the corner; on the other

10   side of the wall she saw, as though through a glass screen, the ravaged kitchen.

'Oh dear,' she said. 'I suppose . . .' and then, hopefully, 'I don't think we could really afford it.'

'Why ever not? You make it sound as though we were on

15   the breadline. We're not short of money just now.' [...]

'I would feel frightfully awkward having someone polishing my floors and things, Henry, I honestly would.' That was a real objection, but he brushed it aside with a snort.

20 The main objection, of course, could not be stated. It was the thought of a daily – or three-mornings-a-week or whatever it was to be – witness to her household disasters. To her failures with the children, to her panics, to her frantic sorties at inappropriate times of

25 day because there was no milk for the baby, no bread, nothing for dinner again. To the fact that she was never quite certain how to work the washing machine, that she was capable of leaving Emma alone in the kitchen with a pan of

30 water boiling on the stove (and had twice done so), that she dithered and forgot and neglected [...]

Henry said, more kindly, 'She could do the worst chores. Give you time for the rest.'

35 And perhaps that was true. Perhaps if there were someone to wash and hoover and do nappies and all that, perhaps then she would be able to keep the shiny things polished as Henry liked, make nicer food, empty ashtrays and

40 plump up cushions before he came home, have clean and ironed shirts ready and available.

She said, 'What do I do?'

From 'Help' by Penelope Lively

Personal response

- These questions will ask for **your** views. The questions may ask:
  - what you learn about a character or relationship or place
  - what your thoughts and feelings are about a character or relationship or place
  - what impressions you get of a character or relationship or place.
- For this type of question, you need to make **comments** about the character or a relationship but then support your views with **evidence** from the passage.
- As you work through the section of text, look at anything the character does or says, since these details will help to form your view about him/her. You may also be told what the character is thinking or feeling. Again, use the character's thoughts and feelings as evidence to support your views.
- If you are asked for your thoughts about a character, try to begin some of your sentences with, 'I think...' or 'I learn...' This will make sure you are focused on giving your views about that person.

 **CD-ROM** ## Sample question and answer

Read the passage below, then read the sample student answer and the examiner's comments that follow.

> Two weeks before Christmas, Angela Hisson gave Mrs Henderson six tickets for the theatre. Mrs Henderson was Angela Hisson's cleaning lady.
>
> 'I wanted to avoid giving you money,' Angela Hisson told
> 5 her. 'Anybody can give money. Somehow the whole process is so degrading. . . taking it. . . giving it. They're reopening the Empire Theatre for a limited season. I wanted to give you a treat. Something you'll always remember.'
>
> Mrs Henderson said, 'Thank you very much.' She had
> 10 never, when accepting money, felt degraded.
>
> Her husband, Charles Henderson, asked her how much Angela Hisson had tipped her for Christmas.
>
> Mrs Henderson said not much. 'In fact,' she admitted, 'nothing at all. Not in your actual pounds, shillings and
> 15 pence. We've got tickets for the theatre instead.'
>
> 'What a discerning woman,' cried Charles Henderson. 'It's *just* what we've always needed.'

'The kiddies will like it,' protested Mrs Henderson. 'It's a pantomime. They've never been to a pantomime.'

20   Mrs Henderson's son, Alec, said *Peter Pan* wasn't a pantomime. At least not what his mother understood by the word. Of course, there was a fairy-tale element to the story, dealing as it did with Never-

25   Never land and lost boys, *but* there was more to it than that. 'It's written on several levels,' he informed her.

'I've been a lost boy all

30   my life,' muttered Charles Henderson, but nobody heard him.

'And I doubt,' said Alec, 'if our Moira's kiddies will make

35   head nor tail of it. It's full of nannies and coal fires burning in the nursery.'

'Don't talk rot,' fumed Charles Henderson. 'They've

40   seen coal fires on television.'

'Shut up, Charlie,' said Alec. His father hated being called Charlie. 'Does it have a principal boy?' asked Mrs Henderson, hopefully. 'Yes and no,' said Alec. 'Not in the sense you mean. Don't expect any

45   singing or any smutty jokes. It's allegorical.'

'God Almighty,' said Charles Henderson.

When Alec had gone out to attend a union meeting, Mrs Henderson told her husband he needn't bother to come to the theatre. She wasn't putting up with him and Alec

50   having a pantomime of their own during the course of the evening and spoiling it for everyone else.

From 'Clap Hands, Here Comes Charlie' by Beryl Bainbridge

Sample question

What do you learn about the characters Mr and Mrs Henderson and their son Alec?   **(10)**

In a question with more than one character, it's important to deal with each one separately, working carefully through the text.

Tip

◀◀ Timing

This was a 10-mark question, so the student should have spent about 13 minutes writing their answer.

Sample answer

> *I think that Mr and Mrs Henderson and their son Alec are a very close family and have very high standards. I don't think they have much money because they were hoping for money off Angela Hisson. Mrs Henderson is her cleaning lady. Mr Henderson asked how much she had been given. 'Charles Henderson asked her how much Angela had tipped her for Christmas.'*
>
> *Charles Henderson also seems very sarcastic. I just think this because he says 'It's just what we've always needed.' He says this in a sarcastic way about the theatre tickets.*
>
> *Overall I think they are a family who work hard to earn money and have very high standards of each other. I also think they are like any other typical family.*

Not correct – there is no supporting evidence for this view.

✓ OK – simple inference.

✓ Simple surface detail.

✓ Inference with textual support.

Weak assertion unsupported by evidence.

Examiner's comments

This is a weak answer that shows the student has not read the passage closely enough. There are some details and comments that would be rewarded but there are points that are incorrect and much of the material in the passage is ignored. The first point is made without any reference to anything that happens in the passage and there is no evidence that they are a 'very close family'. There is some suggestion in the opening dialogue between Charles and Mrs Henderson that they were hoping for money from Mrs Hisson, and there is reward for the simple point that Mrs Henderson is her cleaning lady. The student correctly recognises the sarcasm of Charles Henderson's reply, but the final sentences again drift into vague comments that gain no reward. Notice too that there is no attempt to include anything in the answer about Alec. This answer would be grade E/D.

How to improve this answer

- Tracking the text carefully would have made it easy for the student to improve this answer, because so many points have been missed.
- We learn, for example, that Mrs Henderson accepted the tickets politely, but there is also the clear suggestion that she had never been too proud to accept money as a gift.
- We can also see in the way she explains about the tickets to Charles that she knows he will react negatively. When

he is sarcastic, we see that Mrs Henderson tries to be positive, claiming the grandchildren will enjoy going to the pantomime.

- When Alec gives his view about *Peter Pan*, he appears to be more educated, perhaps even smug or a bit of a 'know-all', and it doesn't take long before he is arguing with Charles. He seems to have little affection for his father and seems to enjoy irritating him by calling him 'Charlie', a name he knows his father hates.

- At the end of the passage, Mrs Henderson seems to become more forceful with her husband, telling him she doesn't want him spoiling the occasion by arguing with Alec.

- Each of these points would have been rewarded.

Your turn!

Now it's your turn to answer this type of question. Read the extract on the next page and answer the question before it. The extract is taken from *Tears of the Giraffe* by Alexander McCall Smith.

What impressions do you get of the jeweller in these lines? (10)

Tips

Track the text line by line, looking carefully at what the jeweller does or says, and what the writer tells you about him.

- If you are not used to doing this type of question, you may find it useful to underline any part of the text that is to do with the jeweller, and then ask yourself, 'What does this tell me about him?'

- Try to use part of the question to begin some of your sentences. For example: 'The first impression I get of the jeweller is…', 'Another impression I get is…'

◀◀ Timing

In the exam, you should try to write an answer in about 13 minutes. However, as you are preparing for the exam, it is better to be accurate than just quick, so make a note of how long it takes you to do a detailed answer. As you improve, you will be able to work more quickly.

The jeweller smiled at them. 'I saw you outside,' he said. 'You parked your car under that tree.'

Mr J. L. B. Matekoni [...] introduced himself, as was polite, and then he turned to Mma Ramotswe.

5 'This lady is now engaged to me,' he said. 'She is Mma Ramotswe, and I wish to buy her a ring for this engagement.' He paused. 'A diamond ring.'

The jeweller looked at him through his hooded eyes, and then shifted his gaze sideways to Mma Ramotswe. She looked

10 back at him, and thought: *There is intelligence here. This is a clever man who cannot be trusted.*

'You are a fortunate man,' said the jeweller. 'Not every man can find such a cheerful, fat woman to marry. There are many thin, hectoring women around today. This one will make you

15 very happy.'

Mr J. L. B. Matekoni acknowledged the compliment. 'Yes,' he said. 'I am a lucky man.'

'And now you must buy her a very big ring,' went on the jeweller. 'A fat woman cannot wear a tiny ring.'

20 Mr J. L. B. Matekoni looked down at his shoes.

'I was thinking of a medium-sized ring,' he said. 'I am not a rich man.'

'I know who you are,' said the jeweller. 'You are the man who owns Tlokweng Road Speedy Motors. You can

25 afford a good ring.'

Mma Ramotswe decided to intervene. 'I do not want a big ring,' she said firmly. 'I am not a lady to wear a big ring. I was hoping for a small ring.'

The jeweller threw her a glance. He seemed

30 almost annoyed by her presence – as if this were a transaction between men, like a transaction over cattle, and she was interfering.

'I'll show you some rings,' he said, bending

35 down to slide a drawer out of the counter below him. 'Here are some good diamond rings.'

He placed the drawer on the top of the counter and pointed to a row of rings nestling in velvet slots. Mr J. L. B. Matekoni caught his breath. The diamonds were set in the

40 rings in clusters: a large stone in the middle surrounded by smaller ones. Several rings had other stones too – emeralds and rubies – and beneath each of them a small tag disclosed the price.

'Don't pay any attention to what the label says,' said

45 the jeweller, lowering his voice. 'I can offer very big discounts.'

From *Tears of the Giraffe* by Alexander McCall Smith

Character response

- Character response questions are focused firmly on the character (or characters) in the passage and how they behave or react, or what they are thinking and feeling.
- Look at anything the character does or says. You may also be told what the character is thinking or feeling.
- You will need to make **comments** about how or why the character behaves in a particular way, or what he or she is thinking, and then support your views with **evidence** from the passage.

Sample question and answer

 CD-ROM

Read the two passages below and on the next page, which are from a short story set in the future. Then read the sample student answer and the examiner's comments that follow.

'Sit down, young man,' said the Official.

'Thanks.' The young man sat.

'I've been hearing rumours about you,' the Official said pleasantly. 'Oh, nothing much. Your nervousness. Your not getting on so well. Several months now I've heard about you, and I
5 thought I'd call you in. Thought maybe you'd like your job changed. Like to go overseas, work in some other War Area? Desk job killing you off, like to get right in on the old fight?'

'I don't think so,' said the young sergeant.

'What *do* you want?'

The sergeant shrugged and looked at his hands. 'To live in peace. To learn that during the
10 night, somehow, the guns of the world had rusted, the bacteria had turned sterile in their bomb casings, the tanks had sunk like prehistoric monsters into roads suddenly made tar pits. That's what I'd like.'

'That's what we'd all like, of course,' said the Official. 'Now stop all that idealistic chatter and tell me where you'd like to be sent. You have your choice – the Western or Northern War
15 Zone.' The Official tapped a pink map on his desk.

But the sergeant was talking at his hands, turning them over, looking at the fingers: 'What would you officers do, what would we men do, what would the *world* do if we all woke tomorrow with the guns in flaking ruin?'

The Official saw that he would have to deal carefully with the sergeant. He smiled quietly.

Now read the second passage on the following page.

> 'Go put your Rust away and forget about it.'
> The sergeant jerked his head up. 'How'd you know I *had* it?' he said.
> 'Had what?'
> 'The Rust, of course.'
> 5 'What're you talking about?'
> 'I *can* do it, you know. I could start the Rust tonight if I wanted to.'
> The Official laughed. 'You can't be serious.'

From 'A Piece of Wood' by Ray Bradbury

Sample question

How does the Official behave towards the sergeant in these lines? **(10)**

Tip

This question asks you to look at the character's behaviour. Look particularly at where the Official's behaviour seems to change or where he acts differently towards the sergeant.

Sample answer

In these lines the Official treats the sergeant with some kind of understanding.✓ He seems to care about the sergeant's welfare, ✓ giving him the choice of war zone to work in. ✓ When the sergeant says he would like to live in peace, the Official agrees ✓ but towards the end of the passage, when the man tells the Official he has the power to turn all the guns to rust, the Official, in a rather worried manner, doubted the genuine authenticity of his claims. ✓

Examiner's comments

This answer makes some sensible comments but could easily have made more use of textual evidence to support what is said. It is also a brief answer that misses out too much detail to earn high marks. This would gain an E grade.

How to improve this answer

- Always try to support any comments with evidence from the passage. For example, at first the Official talks to the sergeant 'pleasantly', and he seems to be trying to put the man at his ease by saying things like, 'I thought I'd call you in'. These quotations support the view made in the answer that the Official seems to care about the man's welfare, and would gain extra marks.
- Work through and comment on everything the Official says to the sergeant. This will show how his behaviour changes towards him – he becomes impatient with him but later he realises 'he would have to deal carefully' with him.
- If the student above had tracked the text more carefully, he or she would have recognised the changes in behaviour more easily.

Your turn!

Now it's your turn to have a go at a 'Character Response'-type question. Read the extract below and answer the question before it.

At the beginning of this extract Mma Ramotswe suggests buying an engagement ring. How does Mr Matekoni react? **(10)**

 Timing

If you have worked through the previous sample questions in this book, you should now be trying to complete a full answer in about 13 minutes.

'...they are talking about our engagement,' she said. 'Some of them even asked to see the ring you had bought me.' She glanced at Mr J. L. B. Matekoni before continuing. 'So I told them that you hadn't bought it yet but that I'm sure that you would be buying it soon.'

5   She held her breath. Mr J. L. B. Matekoni was looking at the ground, as he often did when he felt uncertain.

'A ring?' he said at last, his voice strained. 'What kind of ring?'

Mma Ramotswe watched him carefully. One had to be circumspect with men, when discussing such matters. They had very little understanding of

10   them, of course, but one had to be careful not to alarm them. There was no point in doing that. She decided to be direct. Mr J. L. B. Matekoni would spot subterfuge and it would not help.

'A diamond ring,' she said. 'That is what engaged ladies are wearing these days. It is the modern thing to do.'

15   Mr J. L. B. Matekoni continued to look glumly at the ground.

'Diamonds?' he said weakly. 'Are you sure this is the most modern thing?'

'Yes,' said Mma Ramotswe firmly. 'All engaged ladies in modern circles receive diamond rings these days. It is a sign that they are appreciated.'

Mr J. L. B. Matekoni looked up sharply. If this was true – and it very much

20   accorded with what Mma Potokwane had told him – then he would have no alternative but to buy a diamond ring. He would not wish Mma Ramotswe to imagine that she was not appreciated. He appreciated her greatly; he was immensely, humbly grateful to her for agreeing to marry him, and if a diamond were necessary to announce that to the world, then that was a

25   small price to pay. He halted as the word 'price' crossed his mind [...]

'These diamonds are very expensive,' he ventured. 'I hope that I shall have enough money.'

'But of course you will,' said Mma Ramotswe. 'They have some very inexpensive ones. Or you can get terms . . .'

30   Mr J. L. B. Matekoni perked up. 'I thought that they cost thousands and thousands of pula,' he said. 'Maybe fifty thousand pula.'

'Of course not,' said Mma Ramotswe. 'They have expensive ones, of course, but they also have very good ones that do not cost too much. We can go and take a look. Judgment-day Jewellers, for example. They have a

35   good selection.'

CD-ROM

From *Tears of the Giraffe* by Alexander McCall Smith

The craft of the writer

- This type of question asks you to consider the way the writer has created atmosphere in the story, or how the story affects you as a reader, perhaps by making you anxious about what will happen next.
- The most effective way of tackling these questions is to:
    - look carefully and comment on what happens in the passage
    - comment on the choice of words and phrases the writer uses
    - look for any distinctive ways the story has been organised or structured.
- Avoid 'feature spotting', such as telling the examiner there are a lot of adjectives or short sentences. You will gain no reward for vague or general comments. Always try to give specific examples of the words or phrases you think are important, and then comment on the impact they have on the reader.
- If you are tackling a Foundation Tier paper, you are likely to be asked first of all to explain what happens in the passage and then, for example, how the writer tries to make it tense or exciting. Following the points above will help you gain a good mark.

 CD-ROM

Sample question and answer

Read the passage below, then read the sample student answer and the examiner's comments that follow. The story is set in a future ice age, when London is covered with snow and ice and is deserted, except for one man. He is walking through the streets and pauses when he hears a distant noise. This is what happens next.

> That momentary pause almost cost him his life. Out of a side street, something huge and white moved suddenly into his field of vision. For a moment his mind refused to accept the reality of what he saw: then the paralysis left him and
> 5 he fumbled desperately for his futile revolver. Padding towards him [...] swinging its head from side to side [...] was a polar bear.

He dropped his belongings and ran, floundering over the snow towards the nearest building [...] The Underground
10 entrance was only fifty feet away. The steel grille was closed, but he remembered breaking the lock many years ago. The temptation to look back was intolerable, for he could hear nothing to tell him how near his pursuer was.

For one frightful moment the iron lattice resisted his
15 numbed fingers. Then it yielded reluctantly and he forced his way through the narrow opening [...] The monstrous shape, twice as high as a man [...] reared itself in baffled fury against the grille. The metal bowed but did not yield [...] Then the bear dropped to the ground, grunted softly,
20 and padded away. It slashed once or twice at the fallen haversack, scattering a few tins of food into the snow, and vanished as silently as it had come.

From 'The End of the World' by Arthur C. Clarke

Sample question

Tips

How does the writer make these lines tense and dramatic? (10)

- Stories become tense and dramatic when the events build up and become dangerous, unpredictable or scary for the character involved. In this passage, every detail tells us more about the danger the man is in.

- This is only a short passage so it's important to read everything carefully. Pick out and comment on the key details of what's happening, together with words and phrases that show he's in great danger.

- Your comments about why the lines are tense and dramatic are likely to include words like: danger, urgent, excitement, desperation. To show your reactions to what is happening, your answer is likely to include words and phrases like: feeling tense, worried, unsure about the outcome.

Sample answer

The way the writer makes it seem tense and dramatic is by making the reader fear for the man's life, 'almost cost him his life'. The writer makes everything seem bad for the man which stack the odds of victory on the polar bear's side.

✓ Sensible comment supported by evidence from the text.

Vague general comment not linked to any particular part of the passage.

Although the writer doesn't describe the polar bear it still had dramatic effect by just describing the man's actions. 'refused to accept the reality' and 'fumbled desperately' shows the situation was bad, adding to the tense atmosphere.

✓ Selection of detail is sensible, but the comment that follows is too general.

Incorrect – the polar bear is mentioned in the first paragraph.

The only time the polar bear is mentioned is 'The monstrous shape reared in baffled fury' and 'dropped to the ground, grunted' shows how aggressive and dangerous the bear ✓ was, adding to the tense atmosphere.

✓ Some appropriate selection from the text, although the second quotation is less well linked to the comment.

Examiner's comments

This answer makes some appropriate selection of detail from the passage. It offers one or two sensible comments, although at times the comments are too vague to gain reward. This answer ignores a lot of the small but important detail, and in places it fails to explore how some of the words and phrases help to create tension and drama. This answer would just make it into a D grade.

How to improve this answer

- Tracking the text really carefully is the way to improve this answer, and to look closely at the impact of words and phrases on the reader.
- Look at the second sentence – we are told 'something' appears 'suddenly'. We are not sure what it is and this raises our anxiety because it must be linked to the danger the man is in. Words like 'fumbled desperately' increase the sense of urgency and danger and when we are told his revolver is 'futile' the reader knows the man is struggling to defend himself. As the man desperately tries to outrun the beast, the classic elements of a film chase are included – the desire to look back to see how near the bear is, and the way he struggles to get through the iron gates – so that the reader is never sure he will escape from this 'huge', 'monstrous shape'. Again the impact of these words on the reader can be explored.
- By looking carefully at every part of the passage and considering the impact of words and phrases, you will begin to see how to shape an effective answer.

Your turn!

Now it's your turn to answer this type of question. When you looked at the last section on 'Character Response', you read the extract in which the Official meets a sergeant who suggests he has the power to turn metal into rust. In this second extract, taken from the end of the short story, the Official realises the sergeant has done exactly what he had intended. Read the passage on the following page, and answer the question before it.

What happens in these lines? How does the writer try to make this an exciting ending to the story? (10)

 Timing

Take about 13 minutes to write your own answer to the question.

Then he picked up the phone. 'Mathews,' he said. 'Get off the line, quick.' There was a click of someone hanging up and then he dialled another call. 'Hello, Guard Station, listen, there's a man coming past you any minute now, you

5 know him, name of Sergeant Hollis, stop him, shoot him down, kill him if necessary, don't ask questions, kill the son of a bitch, you heard me, this is the Official talking! Yes, kill him, you hear!'

'But sir,' said a bewildered voice on the other end of the

10 line. 'I can't, I just can't . . .'

'What do you mean, you can't, God damn it!'

'Because . . .' the voice faded away. You could hear the guard breathing into the phone a mile away.

The Official shook the phone. 'Listen to me, listen, get

15 your gun ready!'

'I can't shoot anyone,' said the guard.

The Official sank back in his chair. He sat blinking for half a minute, gasping.

Out there even now – he didn't have to look, no one had

20 to tell him – the hangars were dusting down in soft red rust, and the aeroplanes were blowing away on a brown-rust wind into nothingness, and the tanks were sinking, sinking slowly into the hot asphalt roads, like dinosaurs (isn't that what the man had said?) sinking into primordial* tar pits.

25 Trucks were blowing away in ochre puffs of smoke, their drivers dumped by the road, with only the tyres left running on the highways.

'Sir . . .' said the guard, who was seeing all this, far away. 'Oh, God.'

30 'Listen, listen!' screamed the Official. 'Go after him, get him, with your hands, choke him, with your fists, beat him, use your feet, kick his ribs in, kick him to death, do anything, but get that man. I'll be right out!' He hung up the phone.

35 By instinct he jerked open the bottom desk drawer to get his service pistol. A pile of brown rust filled the new leather holster. He swore and leaped up.

On the way out of the office he grabbed a chair. It's wood, he thought. Good old-fashioned wood, good old-fashioned

40 maple. He hurled it against the wall twice, and it broke. Then he seized one of the legs, clenched it hard in his fist, his face bursting red, the breath snorting in his nostrils, his mouth wide. He struck the palm of his hand with the leg of the chair, testing it. 'All right, God damn it, come on!' he cried.

He rushed out, yelling, and slammed the door.

*primordial – existing at the beginning of time

CD-ROM

From 'A Piece of Wood' by Ray Bradbury

Empathetic response

This type of question tends to appear in Foundation Tier papers. You will be asked to write as if you are the character in the story. You might be asked to write the diary of the character, or perhaps to relate the events of the passage to a neighbour or friend. To gain a good mark, you must:

- imagine yourself as the character, focusing on the key events in the passage that you were involved in
- try to capture the characters' thoughts and feelings as these things happened
- try to make your writing capture the character as much as possible. For example, if the character in the story is a quiet, meek old lady, it would be completely out of character for her to be nasty and unpleasant and start swearing when she tells her friend what happened to her.

Sample question and answer

Read the passage on the following page. In this story, the central character, Jenny, is convinced that her home-help, Mrs Porch, is stealing from her, but she is anxious about how she will be able to deal with the situation. When you have read the passage carefully, read the sample student answer and the examiner's comments that follow.

She felt rather ill and shaky the next day. She tried to avoid Mrs Porch, but she seemed to be everywhere, talking loudly and cheerfully. Once or twice she looked at Jenny with an odd sharpness. 'You feeling all right, dear? You don't look all
5 that good [...] there's a tummy bug about.'

'I'm quite all right,' Jenny said.

Halfway through the morning the bell rang. Mrs Porch [...] said, 'It's the bread man – I'll just pay him, shall I? I can't seem to lay hands on your purse, though, Mrs Taylor – it's
10 not in the usual place.'

Jenny said in a strangled voice, 'It's all right, Mrs Porch, I'll do it.' She got up hastily, spilling the baby's milk as she did so.

'Don't you bother,' said Mrs Porch. 'Ah, there it is.' She
15 reached forward to take the purse from the table beside Jenny, adding... 'Coming, Mr Binns [...]'

'No!' said Jenny shrilly. 'Please leave it, Mrs Porch. I'll pay him myself.'

The baby was crying now, and the bread man ringing the
20 bell again. She left the room hastily.

When she came back, Mrs Porch was soothing the baby. Jenny, her heart thumping horribly, sat down again [...] Mrs Porch said slowly, 'Is there something wrong with the purse, Mrs Taylor? Something bothering you?'

25 'No,' said Jenny wildly. 'At least I don't want – I couldn't bear... There's some sort of mistake, I'm sure, it's just that I felt certain...'

'I see,' said Mrs Porch. She sounded, for a moment, subdued, sad almost, but when she spoke again it was with
30 her old briskness. 'If it was anyone else I'd be very angry, Mrs Taylor, but I've got fond of you, I really have. I like working here, we get on, I thought [...] So we'll keep it between us two, Mrs Taylor, and pretend it never happened, and that's all there is to it [...] unless, of course,' said Mrs
35 Porch, 'you'd rather I didn't come any more?'

After a moment Jenny said, 'No honestly, I . . . I'm sorry, I expect there's been a mistake.'

'Then we'll forget about it. Right?' Mrs Porch gathered up the dirty crockery from the table. As she was leaving the
40 room she turned and said, 'And I'd put the purse back in the dresser, if I were you, Mrs Taylor. It'll be a nuisance if I can't find it, next time the milkman's wanting his money, when you're not about, won't it?'

Jenny said, 'Yes. Yes, all right, Mrs Porch.'

From 'Help' by Penelope Lively

Sample question

Imagine you are Jenny. Write your diary entry for that day. (10)

> Look carefully at what Jenny does and says – this will give you clues about how she is feeling, and help you to decide the kind of things she is thinking about. This will help you capture Jenny's thoughts and feelings in the diary entry. Remember to keep your writing in the first person. **Tip**

> **Timing** This is a 10-mark question, so you should spend about 13 minutes writing your answer.

Sample answer

Well, what a day. Mrs Porch came round as usual making the house look amazingly clean. But I didn't care about the housework today. I cared about Mrs Porch taking my money. Over these past weeks I have become uneasy with Mrs Porch. It's not as if her work is bad, it's just when you have a household worker, you expect them to be trustworthy, not go in your purse and take money when they please. The bread man came today and I wasn't going to let Mrs Porch pinch any more money of mine ✓, so I moved my purse into a different place. When she shouted through to me she couldn't seem to find my purse, I don't know what came over me. I was so mad, confused, I shouted through it's not in the usual place and I got up quickly, spilling all the milk. I'll pay him myself I said to her. I think she knows I'm uneasy with her but I can't bear to lose her. The house will become a terrible mess again. I'll have to see how it goes.

- An attempt here to capture Jenny's feelings.
- ✓ Captures Jenny's indignation at the theft of her money.
- ✓ Builds on the previous sentence – good focus on feelings.
- ✓ Tracks the events.
- ✓ Tracking again is good.
- ✗ Misses all the confrontation.
- Ends weakly, avoiding the ending.

Examiner's comments

This begins well, and captures a sense of Jenny's annoyance at the situation. It shows a good understanding of Jenny's feelings and there is a good selection of detail from the passage. However, the final part of the answer is weak, missing much of what happens when Jenny returns from paying the bread man. It also misses completely the decision Jenny makes to keep Mrs Porch working for her, even though Mrs Porch makes it clear she expects to continue handling, and stealing, the money. Because of the way the answer ends weakly, this answer would be awarded a D grade.

How to improve this answer

- Look more closely at the final part of the passage. Too much is missed in this answer.
- Look for clues in the writing. Jenny answers 'wildly' and cannot complete a sentence – what does that suggest about how she is feeling?
- In the exchange between the two women, ask yourself: who is in control here? How do you know, and how would Jenny feel as this conversation takes place?
- The answer should include what happens in the end. The diary should show how Jenny feels about how the incident turned out.

Your turn!

Now it's your turn to answer this type of question. Read the extract on the following page and answer the question before it. In this extract, a teenage girl, Hannah, is giving an account of the day she and her mother take her grandmother to spend a day at St Alma's, a care home. The family is hoping to organise residential care for 'Grandma', who is suffering from senile dementia.

Imagine you are the mother in the story. When you get home you tell your husband what has happened and how you feel. Write down what you say to him. (10)

Timing ▶▶

Take about 13 minutes to write your answer to the question.

Mum says would I like to go to St Alma's with her when she takes Grandma today. Would I *like* to? Does she mean as a treat? It isn't the sort of outing anyone would *like*, is it? But I say yes. I really should inspect one of these Homes if
5 just to argue better against them. I have never been in one. Mum says St Alma's will not be typical, that it's the best, that she wouldn't dream of suggesting I visited the other place she and Dad looked at. She says I will see immediately how lucky we'll be if we manage
10 to get Grandma into this very wonderful place. She has her fingers crossed [...]
   St Alma's *looks* all right, I suppose. If only Mum would
15 shut up, I'd be quite prepared to notice for myself the attractive house and pleasant gardens, the freshness of the paint and the brightness of the knocker [...]
20 Grandma is quite happy going into St Alma's because I'm on one side and Mum on the other. The floor is very shiny. Grandma says it must've taken
25 some polishing, it's like a skating rink and she's afraid she'll slip. Mum says it isn't in the least
slippy and demonstrates. It's true, the floor only looks slippy but isn't. Grandma refuses to be convinced. Every step we
30 persuade her to take is followed by 'Oh help!' from her. She won't even try to walk properly. She says she should have brought her skates [...] We get her across the hall to the Matron's office and Mum knocks as Grandma asks what in the name of heaven is going on, do we have to knock to get
35 in our own house now.
   I hate the Matron – on sight. She's [...] stiff, smarmy, pretend-kind...Grandma hates the Matron too. Grandma starts sniffing loudly, always a sign of her nervousness. She nudges me, I nudge back. This Matron is exactly the
40 sort of woman who intimidates Grandma [...] I'm not sure about Mum. Mum may not hate this woman, she can't hate her or she wouldn't have brought Grandma here or called St Alma's desirable. But Mum is wary of her, not at all comfortable.

From *Have the Men Had Enough?* by Margaret Forster

Writing

Paper 1 Section B at a glance

You will have to produce two pieces of writing. The first is a piece of description and the second is a piece of personal or narrative writing (i.e. a story).

Advice

- You will have about 65 minutes in total to complete the two tasks.
- You should spend about 25 minutes on the descriptive task and about 40 minutes on the story.
- You should write about one side for the descriptive task and about two sides for the personal/narrative task.
- Both questions are marked out of 20.
- The examiners can give you up to 13 of the marks for what you write (i.e. content) and up to 7 marks for how you write (i.e. spelling, grammar and punctuation).

Descriptive writing

- In this part of the exam paper the emphasis is on description – i.e. **not** telling a story.
- You can only be asked to describe one of the following – **a place**, **an event** or **a person**.
- If you are asked to describe a place, your description could include people as would the description of an event. However, if you are asked to describe a person then the description should focus on that individual.

A place

Sample question and answer

Read the task below, then read the sample student answer and examiner's comments that follow.

Sample question

Describe the scene in a doctor's or dentist's waiting room. (20)

Sample answer

I had to sit for a long time in the waiting room, which seemed like an eternity on the most uncomfortable seat there was, it was like sitting on a thorn bush, the foam of the seat had been riped of and the stapples which held the foam once apon a time stuck into my legs like a knife. I had to sit in a room full of sick people coughing like a volcanoe which was about to explode. Germs and bacteria flying everywhere like fly's around a dustbin. I dreaded the moment every time I had to visit the doctors like death. Every time I go there there is an old lady which I see all the time, she stares at me constantly like she had never seen anything like me before, as if I was from another plant and I feel so uncomfortable around her like using a rock as a pillow. When I have to wait my turn it seems like people have been with the doctor for days, I feel trapped and isolated and there is nowhere to run, nowhere to hide,no one to turn to, its like hell. So I just sit there all to myself waiting for my turn to see the docter whilst listening to the unbearable crying of a baby as if it was possesses thinking it will be over soon lieing to myself to keep myself from going mad.

Examiner's comments

The description is rather brief and unstructured but it is clearly on task. There is a genuine attempt to describe and the description includes individuals. The grade awarded was low D.

How to improve this answer

Addressing the following points would help to improve this answer.

- There has been only a limited attempt to plan or give a structure to the writing.
- Paragraphing would have helped, e.g. a new paragraph after 'a knife'.
- Avoid using the first person 'I'.
- The spelling (there are at least six errors).
- Punctuation. Look at the placing of commas where there should be full stops.
- An incomplete sentence.
- Misuse of the apostrophe.

Your turn!

1. Write an improved version of the answer. Think about its content and organisation as well as technical accuracy.

2. Choose one (or more) of the following tasks and write your own descriptive piece about a place.

   a Describe the scene in a fast-food restaurant.
   b Describe the scene in a doctor's or dentist's waiting room.
   c Describe the scene in a playground of an infants' school at the end of the day.
   d Describe a fish-and-chip shop on a busy Friday evening.
   e Describe a busy market.

Timing

You should spend about 25 minutes writing your own descriptive task.

Tip

Make your description as real as possible. Draw on your own experience. Ask yourself 'What is a fish-and-chip shop **really** like on a Friday night?'

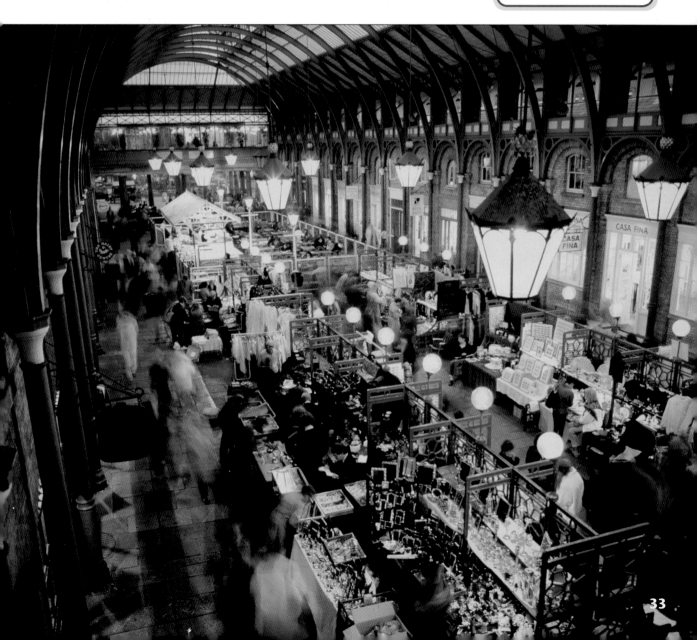

An event

Sample question and answer

Read the task below, then read the sample student answer and examiner's comments that follow.

Sample question

Describe a sporting or musical event. (20)

Sample answer

'GO ON UNITED!' a drunken hooligan belts out to his team. The one half of the stadium was covered with red as if a tall giant just bled to death and all the blood was splattered onto them. The other half was black and white like the olden films with their silent movies.

Terrible teens were pushing and shoving the people in front to get a better view. Drunken, overweight single men are singing their team's songs to try and give them their support. As prepared Policemen are at the ready to solve any little fool wanting to cause caos, medics are helping anyone in need of help.

Fans are bashing anything they could find to help make more noise for their teams. While they're singing and shouting support for the players. The stench of the fatty foods smothered the air while the maniac men managed to excrete their poison out of their mouths. Cleaners are struggling to find time to tidy up this dump but they keep on trying anyway.

Young students are trying to sell sweets and popcorn to little toddlers to gain some extra cash. Programs are being sold by the 64 year old dropout. Overall, I'd say this place needed some improvement on the rubbish and they should try and control the troublemaking teenager and the holligan men causing caos in the stadium.

Examiner's comments

This was awarded a grade D. It isn't always written in sentences; the word choice isn't always effective. Not all of the choice of detail is suitable and it does not always sound real. Plus there are technical errors.

How to improve this answer

Let's just look at the first paragraph. There is an attempt to start in a lively fashion. The image of the giant is exaggerated and doesn't really work. That needs to be rewritten, as does the cinema image. Can you think of a more effective comparison?

As we look further on in the description we see more exaggeration and some poor choice of details. Would there be toddlers at an event like this? Would cleaners be working during the match? The piece ends rather tamely. The answer does not go in 'close'. It is too general, such as when it writes about 'cleaners' and 'teens'.

The real problem is that the work has not been thought out properly and it is all a bit messy. There are errors and there is carelessness. But it could easily be improved. Better planning, better choice of details and greater care taken with spelling, grammar and punctuation will improve this answer from a D to a C and beyond.

Your turn!

Choose one of the titles below and spend about 25 minutes planning and writing your piece.

1. **Describe a sporting or musical event.** (20)

2. **Describe the scene at the first day of the sales.** (20)

Tips

- Make your description as real as possible. Choose your details carefully.

- Remember that 13 marks are awarded for content and 7 marks for spelling, grammar and punctuation.

A person
Sample question and answer

Read the task below, then read the sample student answer and examiner's comments that follow.

Sample question

Describe a person who has been important in your life. (20)

Sample answer

My mother is a very important person in my life as she is always there for me when I get home from school stood by the oven with her red and white oven gloves on with my food in her hands, and as I walk upstairs to get changed all of my washing is folded neatly into piles for me only to mess up again as I take what I want to wear and leave the rest there, and as I get changed my mother will shout me for my food. When I arrive at the table she will ask me if I want anything else with my food such as a drink. All of this may seem to be simple but when you get it altogether it is a lot of work to do. Every morning I get up with my school uniform on my radiator nice and warm for me when I put it on, I walk downstairs to find my money on the table ready for me to take to school, so when she asks me to go down the shop for a loaf of bread or milk it's not a lot to do when you consider what my mother does for me. My mother is a very kind and caring person who is very important to me. I may not like some of the things she does, but I can't complain because she'll only complain back.

Examiner's comments

It's an affectionate description and is quite accurately written.
It is of reasonable length (about a page of writing). It was
awarded a C grade but could have gone higher with a bit more
planning and attention to detail.

How to improve this answer

Why do you think that it is not worth more? Make notes
on what could have improved the answer. Think about the
following.

- How could the shape of the piece be improved?
- Would paragraphing have helped the student to have
  organised it better?
- Could something be done about the first long sentence?
- How could the piece have been made a bit more interesting
  for the reader?
- Could the writer have provided a bit of physical description?

Your turn!

Write an answer to one (or more) of the following tasks.

1. **Describe one of your relatives.** (20)
2. **Describe one of your friends.** (20)
3. **Describe a local character.** (20)

Remember to do the following.

- Describe a real person.
- Draw on your own experience.
- Plan what you want to say and organise your work.
- Try to make it interesting.
- Think carefully about your choice of adjectives and
  adverbs.

Tip

This is a description **not**
a story. Focus carefully on
the details which will bring
the description to life.

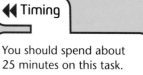

◀◀ Timing

You should spend about
25 minutes on this task.

Personal or narrative writing

Key revision points

Read all the titles carefully and then ask yourself – which one of these can I do best?

- Here you will be offered five titles from which you will be asked to choose just one.
- You will have about 40 minutes to complete the work.
- There are four different types of title:
  - continue a story
  - complete a story
  - autobiographical
  - open title.
- Decide on the one that suits you best before starting to write, then think carefully about what you intend to say. You can, if you wish to, write a plan of what you intend to include in each paragraph. This can be written in your answer book and you can indicate to the examiner that this is your plan.

Sample question and answer 1

Read the task below, then read the beginning and ending to a sample student answer and the examiner's comments that follow.

Sample question

The Challenge. (20)

Examiner's advice

This could be about a whole range of subjects. This can be about a real or imagined experience. However, often this sort of subject works better when a student draws on something that has happened to them. Choose a time in your life when you faced a challenge. It may not be an important event to others but to you it certainly would have been.

Sample answer (opening and closing paragraph)

It was a disaster, everybody failed from the start, a recovery would have to be spectacular. The Bearshead challenge was tough to say the least a ten mile walk over steep terrain, every team had their problems but nobody gave up the weight of our bags was enough. We started off on the wrong bearing to our checkpoint, not a good start.

[...]

At the end of the competition we ranked fourteenth out of twenty five teams and were pleased with the results but just wished we could have pushed a little bit harder to complete the challenge with more points.

Examiner's comments

The above extracts from a student's answer seem to be quite well organised. The opening indicates what it is going to be about and sets the scene. There is a suitable conclusion – not too long – and there is a sense of the challenge having been concluded. This essay was awarded a C grade but it could have gone higher with a bit more care.

Your turn!

1. Re-write the opening paragraph of the student's answer above, putting in accurate punctuation.

2. Imagine that you had chosen the topic 'The Challenge'. Think of five or six things your response could be about, such as a sporting event or a sponsored activity. Write your list and then choose the subject that will suit you best. Now write your full response.

Remember that you have 40 minutes to complete the task.

Tips

- Of the 20 marks, 7 marks can be awarded for spelling, grammar and punctuation. Being accurate is important.
- Don't forget to write your plan.
  - Think about a good opening paragraph – one that will catch the interest of the reader.
  - Next, decide what you want to say in your middle paragraphs. There might be about three of these.
  - Don't forget your final paragraph which will bring your response to an end.

Sample question 2

Read the task below, together with the examiner's advice – then it's your turn.

Sample question

Write about a time when you had to make a difficult choice. **(20)**

Examiner's advice

This topic does not really present the opportunity to write imaginatively as the first one might do. Here you will need to call on your experience. Again though, there are plenty of possibilities: it might be choosing between friends who have fallen out or it might be choosing between two activities that are on at the same time. Think of some other situations which could be used to answer this topic.

Your turn!

On the previous page you have seen the opening and closing paragraphs to a student response on the topic 'The Challenge'. Now write the opening and closing paragraphs for the following topic.

Write about a time when you had to make a difficult choice. **(20)**

Remember what you need to think about:

- Choose what you are going to write about.

- How will you get the examiner interested in the first paragraph?

- What will each middle paragraph be about? You should aim for three or four of these.

- How will you bring your answer to an end in the final paragraph?

Tip

Always try to keep the reader interested, but remember that you don't have to shock or exaggerate to do that.

Timing

Remember that you have 40 minutes to complete the task.

Sample question 3

Read the type of task below, together with the examiner's advice. Then it's your turn.

Sample question type

Continue the following... **(20)**

[In the exam, you will be given specific guidance here on **what** to continue].

Examiner's advice

This type of question is often used in the exam. You must use the exact words of the title. In the instance of the title 'They had landed safely but none of them knew where they were…' this is a third-person narrative and you should not switch to the first person ('I') in the course of your story i.e. stick to 'they' throughout.

In most cases a subject such as this will be imaginary. It is vital that you don't start writing before you have a pretty good idea as to what you want your story to include and how you intend to bring it to a conclusion. Working this out as you go along can lead to a story that does not hold together very well. Choose incidents and characters carefully so that what you write about will be convincing to the reader.

Your turn!

Have a go at a task of this type. Choose one of the following to continue.

1. Continue the following:
   'I had never liked mobile phones and now I know why…'

2. Write a story which begins with the words:
   'Sam knew there was trouble coming as soon as Mrs Thomas closed the door.'

3. Write a story that begins:
   'I really wish I had not agreed to this, but there was no going back now.'

4. Continue the following:
   'Everyone said you should never go back but I could not resist…'

> - Plan what you intend to include in each paragraph and how you propose to end your story.
> - Remember to take great care with spelling, grammar and punctuation.
> - Aim to write about two sides.
>
> **Tips**

> Remember that you have 40 minutes to complete the task.
>
> **Timing**

Sample question and answer 4

Read the task below, together with the examiner's advice – then read the sample answer.

Sample question

The Longest Day of My Life. (20)

Examiner's advice

This topic requires you to think about a personal experience which fits the title and to write about it. The incident might indeed be dramatic but, very often, the best responses to questions like this record ordinary incidents which at the time seemed to be very worrying.

Sample answer

The Longest Day in My Life

I Stumbled off the scabby old school bus with a slumped posture, an evil thought plagued my mind throughout the bus journey. I peered into my school bag with anticipation. Alas, my nightmare was confirmed, I had forgotten my coursework. I tried to scramble thought inside my mind 'I will pretend to be ill' 'I will say my pet died.' After a few moments of dire concentration I realised I had to face the music. Through my own carelessness.

I walked with a slump to my form class with a frown edged across my lips. I did not greet any teachers I passed, afterall I did not want any un-needed attention from them. Through out registration my eyes beamed at the clock, in my mind the words '2:15 is impending doom' kept repeating. Then I started to say how stupid I was 'how did I forget?' Matthew you fool I dared not mention the word coursework out loud just in case anybody with selective hearing managed to hear me. The school bell rang for the first lesson thankfully my first lesson of the day on a Monday was P.E, My most cherished lesson, I sighed with relief, muttering to myself: yes P.E, that will surely take my mind off of Geography and coursework and my doom! I picked up my pace and raced to the changing rooms, I could not wait for a game of football with the lads. But to my severe disappointment the lesson was cancelled due to the heavy rain. What ever was left of my moral, died at that moment, I dragged myself along with the class peering at any clock I could find, the time was now 11:30. I could not bear it anymore the anger, quilt and fear inside my mind just weighed me down. My doom came closer, after a long lunch break. The bell for afternoon registration rang out. My limbs developed a slight shake as fifth lesson edged closer, and closer. The bell for fifth lesson sounded. The moment I dreaded finally came. I dragged myself to the Geography room, I opend the door and was struck by a paper ball. People were chanting 'Free Lesson' and I was gob smacked amazement was not the word for it, could have started crying in joy. After a day of anguish and despair, my Geography teacher was ill. All that worry for nothing. I paused and ponderd for a moment, reflecting back on the day, I giggled.

Examiner's comments

It is long enough and is relevant to the topic. The tension is built up quite well and there is some good vocabulary. It has quite an effective ending – certainly better than '…then I woke up.' Overall it is just worth a C grade.

How to improve this answer

It could have been organised better – by using more paragraphs, for example. The spelling isn't too bad but there are mistakes. Sentence control is not good. In particular there are commas where there should be full stops. However, it could quite easily be improved.

Your turn!

Without changing the basic story, re-write the above student's response in a way that will persuade the examiner to give it a higher grade.

◀◀ Timing

Remember that you have 40 minutes to complete the task.

Sample question 5

Read the task below, together with the examiner's advice – then it's your turn.

Sample question

Write a story which ends: 'She could laugh now, but it was certainly not funny at the time.' **(20)**

Examiner's advice

Here it is vital that you reach the sentence which is your 'destination' effectively. Often examiners complain that not enough planning has gone into essays of this type and students have carried on writing because they do not know how to finish or have tacked on an ending which does not really fit with what has gone before.

Your turn!

Choose one (or more) of the following and write your own ending to the story. **(20)**

1. Write a story which ends with the following:
   '*…and now it really was clear that you could not trust anyone, least of all your friends.*'

2. Write a story which ends with these words: '*Just at that moment, I heard the car draw up outside and I knew I was in deep, deep trouble.*'

3. Write a story which ends with the following:
   My mother looked at me and said, 'I told you it would never work'. I realise now that she was absolutely right.

- You could write a plan for each of these three titles, then choose the one that you feel will produce the best essay.

- Once you've chosen your story, plan your 'route' carefully. Time spent on planning will save you time when you come to write.

- What you write has to lead up to your final sentence and tie in with it.

Tips

◀◀ Timing

Remember that you have 40 minutes to complete this task.

Reading

Paper 2 Section A at a glance

Below are some examples of the types of questions you could be asked in Section A of your Paper 2 exam. These will help you to understand what you are preparing for as you work through this section of the book.

Type 1: Locating and retrieving information

- List reasons or details/Make a list of...
- According to this text or writer, how or what or why...
- Explain how and/or why...

Type 2: Impressions and images

- What impression do you get of the writer/an organisation/people?
- What image does this text create of the writer/an organisation/people?

Type 3: Viewpoint and attitude

- What are the writer's attitudes to...
- What are the writer's opinions of...
- What are the writer's thoughts and feelings about...

Type 4: Intended audience

- Who is this text aimed at?

Type 5: Analysis of persuasive techniques

- How does the writer try to encourage/interest/argue?
- How does this text try to persuade/sell/influence?

Type 6: Comparison of texts

- Compare and contrast these texts.
- Using information from both texts, explain why...

Locating and retrieving information

'Listing details' or 'Finding evidence' questions

Key revision points

- Sometimes this type of question can be answered in bullet point form.
- This type of question is normally just 'search and find' but it may involve some inference.
- When you are asked to 'list' or 'make a list', use bullet or numbered points.
- Make sure that each point is clear and makes sense.
- Make sure that you are thorough and include enough points. The mark allocation will guide you as to how many points you need.

Tip

Inference is when you have to use details from a text to reach conclusions which you are not told directly. It is really reading between the lines. For example, if a man slammed his fist on a table, you would infer that he was angry.

Sample question and answer

Read the passage on the following page taken from *A Walk in the Woods* by Bill Bryson. Then read the sample student answer and examiner's comments that follow.

Now here's a thought to consider. Every twenty minutes on the Appalachian Trail, Katz and I walked further than the average American walks in a week. For 93 per cent of all trips outside the home, for whatever distance or whatever purpose, Americans now get in a car. That's ridiculous.

5   When we moved to the States one of the things we wanted was to live in a town, where we could walk to the shops and post office and library. We found such a place in Hanover, New Hampshire. It's a small, pleasant college town, with a big green, leafy residential streets, an old-fashioned main street. Nearly everyone in town is within an easy level walk of the centre, and yet almost no-one walks anywhere ever for anything. I have a neighbour who

10 drives 800 yards to work. I know another – a perfectly fit woman – who will drive 100 yards to pick up her child from a friend's house. When school lets out here, virtually every child gets picked up and driven from a few hundred yards to three-quarters of a mile home. (Those who live further away get a bus.) Most of the children sixteen years or older have their own cars. That's ridiculous too. On average the total walking of an American these days – that's

15 walking of all types – adds up to 1.4 miles a week, barely 350 yards a day.

At least in Hanover we can walk. In many places in America now, it is not actually possible to be a pedestrian, even if you want to be. I had this brought home to me in Waynesboro [...] when I left Katz at a launderette [...] and set off to find some insect repellent for us. [...]

20 Lots of shops were dark and bare, and there was nowhere I could find to get insect repellent, but a man outside the post office suggested I try K-mart.

'Where's your car?' he said, preparatory to giving directions.

'I don't have a car.'

That stopped him. 'Really? It's over a mile, I'm afraid.'

25 'That's OK.'

He gave his head a little dubious shake, as if disowning responsibility for what he was about to tell me. 'Well, then what you want to do is go up Broad Street, take a right at the Burger King and keep on going. But, you know, when I think about it, it's *well* over a mile – maybe a mile and a half, mile and three quarters. You walking back as well?'

30 'Yeah.'

Another shake. 'Long way.'

'I'll take emergency provisions.'

If he realised this was a joke he didn't show it.

'Well, good luck to you,' he said.

From *A Walk in the Woods* by Bill Bryson

Tip

This question says 'list'. This means you can answer in a paragraph or use bullet points. If the question does not say 'list' it would be sensible to write in paragraphs only.

Sample question

List ten examples from the passage which show that Bill Bryson thinks Americans have a 'ridiculous' attitude towards walking. **(10)**

Sample answer

- *Americans use the car for 93% of all trips.*
- *Most children have cars.*
- *A perfectly fit woman will sometimes drive 100 yards.*
- *The fact that she is 'fit' emphasises how lazy Americans are.*
- *A man seems shocked at the idea of walking a mile.*
- *Americans will do anything to avoid walking.*

Examiner's comments

This answer does make a selection of points from the passage and it would pick up a reasonable mark. However, questions like this are an opportunity to score well and you must not be satisfied with a 'reasonable' mark. The question asked for ten examples and this only provides six bullet points, giving a maximum mark of six. Some points could be made more fully. The second bullet point is carelessly expressed and an easy mark is therefore lost. Most children do not have cars, although most children **aged sixteen and over** do have cars. The final bullet point is a rather general comment and not really an example, although it might have been rewarded. That gives a mark which is just into grade C.

How to improve this answer

You need to keep the question clearly in your mind (you are looking for examples of 'ridiculous' attitudes to walking) and you need to be thorough (you must find ten examples). Work methodically through the passage, looking for every relevant point.

Tips

- Be methodical, relevant and thorough.
- Remember that bullet points should make sense.

Your turn!

Now it's your turn to answer this type of question. Read the extract on the next page and answer the question before it. The extract is taken from a fact sheet produced by The Captive Animals' Protection Society (CAPS).

List the criticisms which CAPS makes of zoos. (10)

Timing

You should not spend more than 13–14 minutes on this question. If you can do it quickly you will gain some time for the other questions.

Sad Eyes and Empty Lives

In the wild, animals react to their surroundings, avoiding predators, seeking food and interacting with others of their species – doing what they have evolved
5 for. Consequently, even what might seem 'larger' or 'better' enclosures may be [...] impoverished in terms of the animals' real needs.

Frustration and boredom are commonplace amongst
10 animals in zoos and can lead to obsessive and repetitive behaviours in the form of pacing, swaying, and even self-mutilation. This is known as stereotypic behaviour and such pointless, repetitive movements have also been noted in people with mental illnesses. With nothing to do, animals in
15 zoos go out of their minds. Disturbed maternal behaviour may involve over-grooming and the rejection or killing of young. [...]

Even diets are unnatural, with zebras in zoos becoming overweight as the grass they are given is higher in calories
20 than the grasses of the African savannah. The resulting obesity can affect fertility. [...]

Some animals suffer such serious behavioural problems in zoos that they are given anti-depressants, tranquillisers and anti-psychotic drugs to control their behaviour.
25 Zoos often refer to the animals they confine as being 'ambassadors' of their species, but just what message does it give when we see animals in such unnatural conditions, displaying disturbed behaviours?

From *The Captive Animals' Protection Society*

'Explain' questions

Key revision points

- This type of question tests your ability to understand and follow an argument.
- You need to be clear and coherent, following the text in a logical sequence.
- Select the key points and quotations and try to weave them into your answer.

CD-ROM ⟶ ## Sample question and answer

Read the passage on the next page, then read the sample student answer and examiner's comments that follow.

> The industrial towns of the North are ugly because they happen to have been built at a time when modern methods of steel-construction and smoke-abatement were unknown, and when everyone was too busy making money to think about anything else. They go on being ugly largely because the Northerners have got used to that kind of thing and do not notice
> 5   it. Many of the people in Sheffield or Manchester, if they smelled the air along the Cornish cliffs would probably declare that it had no taste in it. But since the war, industry has tended to shift southward and in doing so has grown almost comely. The typical post-war factory is not a gaunt barrack or an awful chaos of blackness and belching chimneys; it is a glittering white structure of concrete, glass and steel, surrounded by green lawns and beds of tulips.
> 10   Look at the factories you pass as you travel out of London [...]; they may not be aesthetic triumphs but certainly they are not ugly in the same way as the Sheffield gasworks.

From *The Road to Wigan Pier* by George Orwell

Sample question

Explain why and how industry in the north of England is different from industry in the south of England, according to Orwell.   **(10)**

Sample answer

In these lines Orwell is describing the differences of the North of England to the South. The way in which he does this is very one-sided. He only says all the good points for the South, but all the bad things for the North.

On line 25, he is giving us an explanation of why the northern industrial towns are so 'ugly'. His main reason is because of the time. Orwell gives the impression that Northerners did not care about their environment because 'everyone was too busy making money'. This could have offended northerners.

Orwell points out a difference of smell. He says that 'people in Sheffield or Manchester, if they smelled the air along the Cornish cliffs would probably declare it had no taste in it. Orwell is judging people before he knows them, and these people would just notice a difference in the air.

Orwell then goes on to saying how industry has 'grown almost attractive' just because it has moved south. I believe that Orwell is trying to point out a major difference which he believes that industry in the north is ugly and polluted, whereas in the south it becomes attractive. Orwell is being very prejudice in these lines as whether industry is in the north or the south it would still be the same.

Annotations:

The first sentence of this answer is not necessary and would gain no credit.

The second sentence is not answering the question and the answer is beginning to attack Orwell rather than analyse his argument.

The third sentence makes a general point but again the focus is uncertain.

A whole paragraph is not really gaining much, if any, credit.

The final sentence criticises Orwell rather than explains what he is saying.

Examiner's comments

Personal feelings are getting in the way here and too much of the answer is irrelevant or wrong. The answer lacks clarity and detail. It would be marked as grade E.

How to improve this answer

You need to keep the question firmly in mind and focus on what Orwell is saying to explain 'why' and 'how' he thinks industry is different in the north and the south. It would help to make the essential contrast first, establishing that Orwell thinks that industry in the north is 'ugly' while industry in the south is 'almost attractive'. There are two areas to explore and the next section of your answer should explain the reasons **why** industry in the north is ugly. The final section of your answer should then focus on the reasons why industry in the south is more attractive. Using paragraphs to give your answer some shape and structure will allow you to present your answer clearly.

> **Tips**
>
> - Do not waste time and words. Every sentence should be making a point which will gain a tick.
> - Follow the writer's argument step by step, selecting relevant material.
> - Use your own words where you can.

> **Timing** ▶▶
>
> You should take no more than 13–14 minutes to answer this question.

Your turn!

Now it's your turn to answer this type of question. Read the extract opposite and answer the question before it. The extract is also taken from the fact sheet produced by The Captive Animals' Protection Society (CAPS).

According to CAPS, why are zoos not helping in the conservation of animals? (10)

The 'con' in conservation?

A quarter of British zoos don't keep any threatened species and those that do only have them in very small numbers. Many animals are there just to draw in the tourists.

5 Many of the high-profile, co-ordinated breeding programmes amongst zoo bodies have no mechanism for returning animals to the wild, they simply provide for the continued breeding of certain species.

When reintroduction programmes do take place they are
10 often initiated by government wildlife agencies rather than by zoos. Many examples given by zoos as 'success stories' have simply been translocations into previously occupied or vacant habitat or have failed to lead to the establishment of a self-sustaining wild population.

15 Captive-bred animals often lack survival skills, especially those normally learned from a parent – finding food, avoiding predators, etc. Some reintroduction projects have had to be suspended indefinitely.

Releases of captive animals also pose a significant
20 disease threat to native populations. In some cases reintroductions have been cancelled after discovering viruses in captive-bred populations that were due to be released in areas where the virus was unknown; in others, native animals have died because of viruses spread by
25 introduced animals.

Zoos still take animals from the wild. Throughout the 1990s over 1,000 elephants were taken from the wild and sold to zoos and circuses and over 70% of elephants in European zoos were wild caught.

30 It is estimated to be 50 times more expensive to keep an elephant in a zoo than to protect sufficient natural habitat to sustain that elephant and many other animals. Major conservation groups do not think that captive breeding contributes significantly to elephant conservation and
35 that priority should instead be placed on establishing more protected areas and enforcing anti-poaching legislation.

CD-ROM

From *The Captive Animals' Protection Society*

Impressions and images

Key revision points

- Impressions are the effects produced in your mind.
- You need to think about and use the text to reach impressions.
- You must cover the text thoroughly and methodically.
- You should include at least five or six impressions, all of them linked to evidence.

 **Sample question and answer**

Read the extract below. Then read the sample student answer and examiner's comments that follow. This extract was written by George Orwell in 1937 after he visited the industrial north of England.

Sheffield, I suppose, could justly claim to be called the ugliest town in the Old World: its inhabitants, who want it to be pre-eminent in everything, very likely do make that claim for it. It has a population of half a million and it contains fewer decent buildings than the average East Anglian village of five hundred. And the stench! If at rare moments you stop
5   smelling sulphur it is because you have begun smelling gas. Even the shallow river that runs through the town is usually bright yellow with some chemical or other. Once I halted in the street and counted the factory chimneys I could see; there were thirty-three of them, but there would have been far more if the air had not been obscured
10   by smoke. One scene especially lingers in my mind. A frightful patch of waste ground [...] trampled bare of grass and littered with newspapers and old saucepans. To the right an isolated row of gaunt four-roomed houses, dark red, blackened by smoke. To the left an
15   interminable vista of factory chimneys, chimney beyond chimney, fading away into a dim blackish haze. Behind me a railway embankment made of the slag from furnaces. In front, across the patch of waste ground, a [...] building of red and yellow brick [...].
20   At night, when you cannot see the hideous shapes of the houses and the blackness of everything, a town like Sheffield assumes a kind of sinister magnificence. Sometimes the drifts of smoke are rosy with sulphur, and serrated flames, like circular saws, squeeze themselves out [...] of the foundry chimneys. Through the open doors of foundries you see fiery serpents of iron being hauled to and fro by redlit boys, and you hear the whiz and
25   thump of steam hammers and the scream of the iron under the blow.

From *The Road to Wigan Pier* by George Orwell

Sample question

What impressions do you get of Sheffield? (10)

Sample answer

> Orwell describes Sheffield as 'the ugliest town in the world'. He says there are few 'decent buildings'. The town smells bad with 'the stench' of 'sulphur' and the river is usually 'bright yellow' with chemicals. Sheffield has at least 'thirty three chimneys' which bellow out smoke. Orwell believes the waste ground is even worse than London. There is lots of rubbish around and it is littered with 'newspapers and old saucepans'. Even the railway embankment is made from 'slag'.

Tip

Remember to use the words of the question as your 'way in' to your answer. For example, in this answer you could start with: 'I get the impression that...'

Examiner's comments

This answer is quite brief and, although it picks out some useful details from the text, it is not really using those details to reach 'impressions'. The only time it does this is when it says 'it smells bad'. A lot of the problem here comes from not using the words of the question to get the focus right. It also stops too soon and fails to mention the 'hideous' houses or the noise or the 'fiery serpents' which give an impression of hell. This answer would reach grade D.

How to improve this answer

The answer would be better if it started with 'I get the impression that...' It needs to make it clear what impressions are created by the details from the text. For example, the 'thirty three chimneys' give the impression that Sheffield is an industrial town. It is not difficult to use the 'yellow river' and the air full of smoke to reach the impression that it is very polluted.

Some obvious details could be included, such as the impression that Sheffield is a large town with a population of half a million.

You should spend no more than 13–14 minutes on this question.

Timing ▶▶

Tips

- Do not waste time and words. Every sentence should be making a point which will gain a tick.

- Follow the writer's argument step by step, selecting relevant material.

- You must link your impressions to evidence in the text.

- Use your own words where you can.

Your turn!

Now it's your turn to answer this type of question. Read the extract below and answer the question before it.

What impressions do you get of zoos from this extract? (10)

Zoos claim that seeing a live wild animal gives an unparalleled appreciation of the power and wonder of nature, but what are they really showing us?

5   TV wildlife programmes have ensured that our understanding of these animals extends beyond these pathetic exhibits. Indeed, CAPS believes school trips to zoos leave children with a distorted view of wildlife.

Signs on zoo enclosures can often give little information, or even incorrect details. A [...] study [...] in the UK found
10   41% of the individual animals on display had no signs identifying their species – the most basic of information.

Studies have shown that most visitors spend
15   less than three minutes looking at each exhibit, and sometimes as little as eight seconds.
20   Zoos claim that they afford people the opportunity to see something that many will never see in the wild. This is true; we will have
25   to make do with books, magazines and television. However, can a few minutes of entertainment ever justify the tragedy of disturbed behaviours and suffering we have outlined?

Some zoos even present animals performing little more than circus tricks to keep the visitors amused. CAPS have
30   filmed elephants, sea lions and parrots performing tricks at several British zoos. We even uncovered electric goads being used on elephants during training.

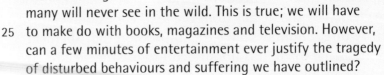

From *The Captive Animals' Protection Society*

Viewpoint and attitude

Key revision points

- This type of question is asking you to work out the views or opinions of the writer.
- You need to think about and use the text to work out the writer's views and opinions.
- You must cover the text thoroughly and methodically.
- Be prepared to look for a range of views and opinions.

Sample question and answer

Read the extract below, then read the sample student answer and examiner's comments that follow. This extract was written by George Orwell in 1937 after he visited the industrial north of England.

> The industrial towns of the North are ugly
> because they happen to have been built
> at a time when modern methods of steel-
> construction and smoke-abatement were
> 5 unknown, and when everyone was too busy
> making money to think about anything else.
> They go on being ugly largely because the
> Northerners have got used to that kind of thing
> and do not notice it. Many of the people in
> 10 Sheffield or Manchester, if they smelled the air
> along the Cornish cliffs would probably declare that it had
> no taste in it. But since the war, industry has tended to shift
> southward and in doing so has grown almost comely. The
> typical post-war factory is not a gaunt barrack or an awful
> 15 chaos of blackness and belching chimneys; it is a glittering
> white structure of concrete, glass and steel, surrounded by
> green lawns and beds of tulips.

From *The Road to Wigan Pier* by George Orwell

Sample question

What are Orwell's thoughts and feelings about industry in the north and the south of England? (10)

Remember to use the words of the question as your 'way in' to your answer. For example, 'So, Orwell thinks that…'

Tip

55

Sample answer

> In these lines Orwell is describing the differences of the North of England to the South. The way in which he does this is very one-sided. He only says all the good points for the South, but all the bad things for the North.
>
> He gives us an explanation of why the northern industrial towns are so 'ugly'. His main reason is because of the time. Orwell gives the impression that Northerners did not care about their environment because 'everyone was too busy making money'. This could have offended northerners.
>
> Orwell points out a difference of smell. He says that 'people in Sheffield or Manchester, if they smelled the air along the Cornish cliffs would probably declare it had no taste in it.' Orwell is judging people before he knows them, and these people would just notice a difference in the air.
>
> Orwell then goes on to saying how industry has 'grown almost attractive' just because it has moved south. I believe that Orwell is trying to point out a major difference which he believes that industry in the north is ugly and polluted, whereas in the south it becomes attractive. Orwell is being very prejudice in these lines as whether industry is in the north or the south it would still be the same.

Examiner's comments

This answer (which is the same as the answer on page 49) does show some understanding of what Orwell is saying about industry in the north and the south but a lot of relevant detail from the text is missed. The **focus** of the answer is also very uneasy as it does not adapt to the specific question. It does not stick to **Orwell's thoughts and feelings** and the student cannot resist the temptation to comment on his views. The third paragraph reveals some misunderstanding of the text. This answer would probably reach grade D.

How to improve this answer

The answer would be better if it started with 'Orwell thinks…' and most, if not all, of the sentences should also use the words of the question. It would also be sensible to organise the answer into two paragraphs, one dealing with his thoughts and feelings about the north and one dealing with the south. A good answer would 'disentangle' the text.

Your turn!

Now it's your turn to answer this type of question. Read the extract below and answer the question before it.

What are Bill Bryson's thoughts and feelings about Blackpool? (10)

You should spend no more than 13–14 minutes on this question.

◀◀ Timing

Tips

- Do not waste time and words. This question is not asking for your views.

- Follow what the writer is saying step by step, selecting relevant material.

- Each thought or feeling needs to be clearly linked to evidence in the text.

- Use the words of the question as your 'way in'.

Blackpool – and I don't care how many times you hear this, it never stops being amazing – attracts more visitors every year than Greece and has more holiday beds than the whole of Portugal [...].

5   Whatever you may think of the place, it does what it does very well – or if not very well at least very successfully. In the past twenty years, during a period in which the number of Britons taking traditional seaside holidays has declined by a fifth, Blackpool has increased
10   its visitor numbers by 7per cent and built tourism into a £250-million-a-year industry – no small achievement when you consider the British climate, the fact that Blackpool is ugly, dirty and a long way from anywhere, that its sea is an open toilet, and its attractions nearly all
15   cheap, provincial and dire.

It was the illuminations that had brought me there. I had been hearing and reading about them for so long that I was genuinely keen to see them. So, after securing a room in a modest guesthouse
20   on a back street, I hastened to the front in a sense of some expectation. Well, all I can say is that Blackpool's illuminations are nothing if not splendid, and they are not splendid. There is, of course, always a danger of disappointment when
25   you finally encounter something you have wanted to see for a long time, but in terms of letdown it would be hard to exceed Blackpool's light show. I thought there would be lasers sweeping the sky, strobe lights tattooing the clouds and other
30   gasp-making dazzlements. Instead there was just a rumbling procession of old trams decorated as rocket ships or Christmas crackers, and several miles of paltry decorations on lampposts. I suppose if you had never seen electricity in action,
35   it would be pretty breathtaking, but I'm not even sure of that. It all just seemed tacky and inadequate on rather a grand scale, like Blackpool itself.

From *Notes from a Small Island* by Bill Bryson

Intended audience

Key revision points

- This type of question is only used with advertisements.
- It is asking you to identify who exactly a text is aimed at.
- You will probably need to think about the pictures as well as the words.
- Think about how advertisers target people by age, gender and interest.

> Remember that this question is asking 'who' the leaflet is trying to attract. It is not asking 'how' it attracts.
>
> **Tip**

Sample question and answer  CD-ROM

Read the leaflet below and on the following page, then the sample student answer and examiner's comments that follow. The leaflet was intended to attract visitors to the city of Sheffield.

Sample question

Who is this leaflet trying to attract to Sheffield? (10)

Whether you're visiting Sheffield for a few hours or several days you're sure to find something of interest just around the next corner!

With award-winning museums and galleries, a remarkable industrial heritage and some of the best international sports facilities in the UK, there is a huge variety of things to enjoy. Add to this our acclaimed nightlife, excellent shopping and enviable programme of world class theatre and music, and you are spoilt for choice!

England's fourth largest city is a great place to visit. We hope that this guide will give you some ideas on what to see and do... apart from enjoying the friendly Sheffield welcome of course!

Sheffield...

Gardens and Open Spaces

With over 150 woodlands and 50 public parks, Sheffield is England's greenest city. The city centre boasts the stylish Peace Gardens and the magnificent Winter Garden – home to more than 2500 plant species from all over the world! Why not take a trip out to the Sheffield Botanical Gardens to see the wonderful Victorian Pavilions and discover the exotic plant collection?

- Winter Garden
  Surrey Street, Sheffield, S1.
  Tel: 0114 221 1900.
  Open daily. Admission free.

- Peace Gardens
  Pinstone Street, Sheffield, S1.
  Tel: 0114 273 6895.
  Open daily. Admission free.

- Botanical Gardens
  Clarkehouse Road, Sheffield, S10.
  Tel: 0114 267 6496.
  Open daily. Admission free.

An Hour in Sheffield

Even if you only have an hour to spare you can still enjoy some of the city centre sights! The Winter Garden makes a great starting point for a walking tour. Take in the beautiful architecture of the theatres, the Cathedral of St Peter and St Paul, the Town Hall and Sheffield City Hall or stroll through one of the city's art galleries.

Shopping

The city centre, along Fargate, the Moor and Orchard Square, is home to numerous well-known retail brands. Independent stores and boutiques can be found in the Devonshire Quarter and along Ecclesall Road and for those looking for the more unusual purchase, why not visit the antiques quarter on Abbeydale Road? Sheffield is also fortunate to have one of Europe's largest shopping malls a short Supertram ride from the city centre. With more than 270 shops, Meadowhall is a shopper's paradise.

- City Centre
  General opening Monday – Saturday.
  9am – 5.30pm, Sunday varies.

- Meadowhall
  Tel: 0845 600 6800. Open daily, times vary.

Sample answer

This leaflet is trying to attract everyone to Sheffield. They do this by having lots of different range of activities for everyone, so they give the impression that anyone and everyone would like it there. The pictures are bright and colourful, so this makes the leaflet eye catching to people looking for a place of fun and excitement. They include pictures of clubbing, sports, boats, big shopping centres views of Sheffield from afar, pictures of buildings that are structurally beautiful, museums and galleries. They use emotive and persuasive language. They tell us lots of information about such attraction in great detail with lots of persuasive language. It gives us lots of ways to get in contact with different places to help us and addresses and phone numbers of places we might like to visit.

Examiner's comments

This answer does get the basic point that the leaflet is trying to attract a wide range of people by mentioning lots of different activities. It is true that the leaflet is attempting to attract people who like fun and excitement, although it is not really the colour of the pictures which does this. The answer lists a range of attractions but then drifts into vague comments about 'emotive' and 'persuasive' language. The last sentence of the answer is irrelevant and the answer loses focus on the question.

This answer gets close to a grade C but it is probably at the top of grade D.

How to improve this answer

This answer needs to identify some of the specific groups of people who are being targeted by the leaflet. For example, the nightlife and sports facilities are attracting young, active people but the museums, galleries and industrial heritage would attract those who are interested in culture and history. The emphasis on shopping is obviously aimed at people who like shopping. People who enjoy music and theatre are also tempted by 'world class' performances. The gardens and green spaces would attract people who enjoy nature and perhaps some peace and quiet. Those who visit for sightseeing can take the walking tour which includes the 'beautiful architecture'.

Tips

- Remember you must identify the specific audiences.
- Be careful not to rush into claiming that leaflets attract 'everyone'.
- Each audience should be clearly linked to evidence from the text.

Timing ▶▶

You should spend no more than 13–14 minutes on this question.

Your turn!

Now it's your turn to answer this type of question. Read the leaflet on Blackpool Zoo (opposite) and answer the question before it.

Who is this leaflet trying to attract to Blackpool Zoo? (10)

GORILLA MOUNTAIN · AWARD-WINNING · LEMUR WOOD

meet the animals

Discover the secrets about our animals that only the keepers know! Our fantastic education team work alongside them to bring you a full programme of exciting talks and feeds throughout the day.

Blackpool Zoo is a great supporter of conservation projects around the world in many endangered habitats.

award-winning animal park

Elephants, gorillas, lions, tigers, orang utans, to name but a few – these are just some of the 400 species of mammals, birds, reptiles and invertebrates living here at Blackpool Zoo in 32 acres of stunning parkland and picturesque lakes. Safe, open spaces, play areas and natural enclosures invite visitors of all ages to enjoy their day at Blackpool Zoo.

ANIMAL DISPLAYS · THEATRE

EXHIBITIONS · AMPLE PARKING · MINIATURE RAILWAY · ANIMAL FEEDS · DINOSAURS

more than just a zoo...

Blackpool Zoo really is a day out for all the family. As well as the amazing animals, there is so much more to do, including browsing in our quality gift shops, dining in our family restaurant, or even enjoying a ride on our miniature railway. A coffee shop, exhibition area and conference room are located in the entrance area, and displays and theatre take place in our outdoor arena.

take a closer look!

education, conservation family fun

FAMILY RESTAURANT · PLAY ZONE · LAKE & PARKLAND SETTING · GIFT SHOPS

Analysis of persuasive technique

- You must look at what is said (content and structure).
- You must look at how it is said (language and tone).
- You should look at pictures and headlines, if relevant.
- This type of question is very common so you must prepare for this.

 **Sample question and answer**

Read the Sheffield leaflet on pages 58–59, then read the sample student answer and examiner's comments below. The leaflet was intended to attract visitors to the city of Sheffield.

Sample question

How does this leaflet try to attract visitors to Sheffield? (10)

Sample answer

This leaflet is filled with fresh and bright colours throughout. 'Sheffield' is written in bold followed by ellipsis which makes the reader want to find out what Sheffield has to offer. This portrays to the reader that people who live in Sheffield are proud of it and this reinforces this idea.

The first paragraph is short and effective, this is combined by the second paragraph which explains what Sheffield has to offer. It covers all target audiences and age groups so everyone is inspired to visit.

The pictures throughout are unique and astonishing – they are so unbelievable that Sheffield looks like a fantasy world full of awe and wonder to amaze all.

Key destinations are stated and their details supplied. This saves a potential visitor having to find this out themselves. The leaflet contains opening times, contact numbers and websites.

The leaflet is cleverly laid out with text in different areas for originality and to interest the reader and easy to read text.

- Remember that this question is asking 'how' the leaflet is trying to attract visitors to Sheffield. It is not asking what makes the leaflet itself attractive.
- It is asking you to analyse how a text tries to achieve its aims. It is not asking you whether it succeeds.
- Remember to say what is in the pictures and, above all, what message they are sending to the reader.

Examiner's comments

This is an example of exactly how **not** to answer this type of question. It is not very likely that anyone would take a trip to Sheffield, or anywhere else, because a leaflet has 'bright' colours. Bold fonts and ellipsis are not persuasive in themselves and the idea that this shows how proud the people of Sheffield are of their city is not very convincing. The vague claim that the first paragraph is 'short and effective' says nothing and, although it is true that that the leaflet is trying to target a wide range of people, there is no detail here. The pictures do try to impress, but this answer does not look closely at any of them. There is no attempt to look at the language of the leaflet, and there is so much to comment on. The final two paragraphs add very little. This is a grade E/F answer.

How to improve this answer

- This answer needs to focus on the detail of the leaflet and avoid getting bogged down in presentational matters. The key is to see that this leaflet is typical of almost all promotional material in stressing how much there is to do in Sheffield. It explicitly mentions 'huge variety' and 'spoilt for choice' and then gives a lot of examples of what exactly is available in the city. It lists things from nightlife to museums and sport to art galleries, which would appeal to almost every interest and age. It also uses impressive statistics such as the 150 woodlands and the 270 shops in Meadowhall.

- The language is positive and seductive, stressing the quality and excellence of the facilities in Sheffield and this answer needs to find words and phrases such as 'shopper's paradise' or 'world class' and comment on them.

- The pictures show people enjoying themselves and illustrate the range of attractions in Sheffield. They present an image of a lively, attractive city with lots of countryside around it.

Your turn!

Now it's your turn to answer this type of question. Read the leaflet on Blackpool Zoo on page 61 and answer the question below.

How does this leaflet try to attract visitors to Blackpool Zoo? (10)

Tips

- Remember to look at 'what is said' and include facts, figures, examples, personal experience or quotations.

- Look at the words and phrases which are used to attract.

- Think about the messages in the pictures.

- You can weave together your comments on content, language and pictures, but you must cover each aspect.

CD-ROM

Timing

You should spend no more than 13–14 minutes on this question.

Comparison of texts

Key revision points

- You must use **both** texts to answer this type of question.
- You must do exactly what you are asked to do.
- You will usually be asked to organise your answer into two or three paragraphs.

CD-ROM ## Sample question and answer

Read the extract by George Orwell below and the Sheffield leaflet on pages 65 and 66. Then read the sample student answer and examiner's comments that follow.

Sheffield, I suppose, could justly claim to be called the ugliest town in the Old World: its inhabitants, who want it to be pre-eminent in everything, very likely do make that claim for it. It has a population of half a million and it contains fewer decent buildings than the average East Anglian village of five hundred. And the stench! If at rare
5   moments you stop smelling sulphur it is because you have begun smelling gas. Even the shallow river that runs through the town is usually bright yellow with some chemical or other. Once I halted in the street and counted the factory chimneys I could see; there were thirty-three of them, but there would have been far more if the air had not been obscured by smoke. One scene especially lingers in my mind. A frightful patch of waste
10   ground [...] trampled bare of grass and littered with newspapers and old saucepans. To the right an isolated row of gaunt four-roomed houses, dark red, blackened by smoke. To the left an interminable vista of factory chimneys, chimney beyond chimney, fading away into a dim blackish haze. Behind me a railway embankment made of the slag from furnaces. In front, across the patch of waste ground, a [...] building of red and
15   yellow brick [...].

    At night, when you cannot see the hideous shapes of the houses and the blackness of everything, a town like Sheffield assumes a kind of sinister magnificence. Sometimes the
20   drifts of smoke are rosy with sulphur, and serrated flames, like circular saws, squeeze themselves out of [...] the foundry chimneys. Through the open doors of the foundries you see fiery serpents of iron being hauled to and
25   fro by redlit boys, and you hear the whiz and thump of steam hammers and the scream of the iron under the blow.

Whether you're visiting Sheffield for a few hours or several days you're sure to find something of interest just around the next corner!

With award-winning museums and galleries, a remarkable industrial heritage and some of the best international sports facilities in the UK, there is a huge variety of things to enjoy. Add to this our acclaimed nightlife, excellent shopping and enviable programme of world class theatre and music, and you are spoilt for choice!

England's fourth largest city is a great place to visit. We hope that this guide will give you some ideas on what to see and do... apart from enjoying the friendly Sheffield welcome of course!

Sheffield

Gardens and Open Spaces

With over 150 woodlands and 50 public parks, Sheffield is England's greenest city. The city centre boasts the stylish Peace Gardens and the magnificent Winter Garden - home to more than 2500 plant species from all over the world! Why not take a trip out to the Sheffield Botanical Gardens to see the wonderful Victorian Pavilions and discover the exotic plant collection?

- Winter Garden
  Surrey Street, Sheffield, S1.
  Tel: 0114 221 1900.
  Open daily. Admission free.

- Peace Gardens
  Pinstone Street, Sheffield, S1.
  Tel: 0114 273 6895.
  Open daily. Admission free.

- Botanical Gardens
  Clarkehouse Road, Sheffield, S10.
  Tel: 0114 267 6496.
  Open daily. Admission free.

An Hour in Sheffield

Even if you only have an hour to spare you can still enjoy some of the city centre sights! The Winter Garden makes a great starting point for a walking tour. Take in the beautiful architecture of the theatres, the Cathedral of St Peter and St Paul, the Town Hall and Sheffield City Hall or stroll through one of the city's art galleries.

Shopping

The city centre, along Fargate, the Moor and Orchard Square, is home to numerous well-known retail brands. Independent stores and boutiques can be found in the Devonshire Quarter and along Ecclesall Road and for those looking for the more unusual purchase, why not visit the antiques quarter on Abbeydale Road? Sheffield is also fortunate to have one of Europe's largest shopping malls a short Supertram ride from the city centre. With more than 270 shops, Meadowhall is a shopper's paradise.

- City Centre
  General opening Monday – Saturday.
  9am – 5.30pm, Sunday varies.

- Meadowhall
  Tel: 0845 600 6800. Open daily, times vary.

Sample question

Compare the impressions of Sheffield given by Orwell's text and the leaflet. **(10)**

Tip

Look carefully at what one text says and then look at the second text.

You should organise your answer into **two** paragraphs using the following headings:

- the impressions of the buildings
- the impressions of the environment.

Sample answer

The leaflet describes 'beautiful architecture', although it does not actually mention the buildings of the city in detail, only by name. This impression is far removed from the one Orwell gives of an 'interminable vista of factory chimneys' and 'hideous shapes of the houses' that are 'blackened by smoke.' The leaflet says 'beautiful', Orwell says 'ugly' – a direct contrast.

While Sheffield apparently boasts '150 woodlands and 50 public parks' making it 'England's greenest city', Orwell's impression of the city was wildly different. The only patch of green that he appeared to notice was 'trampled bare of grass'. The leaflet claims 'numerous opportunities for walking and cycling' in the country but Orwell writes as if the North is entirely made up of factories 'belching smoke'.

Examiner's comments

This answer does not use headings but it is organised into two paragraphs and it is easy to follow. The answer starts with the leaflet and picks up the essential point about the 'beautiful architecture', although it is not clear what is meant by the leaflet mentioning the buildings 'only by name'. The basic contrast is established clearly enough but it could be argued that chimneys are not ideal examples of buildings. The selection of material could be better, and more thorough. As far as the environment is concerned, the basic contrast is fair enough. However, both texts have more to say about the environment and this answer, although reasonable enough, is rather thin. It would probably just reach grade C.

How to improve this answer

The most obvious way to improve this answer is to look for more detail from the texts. For example, the leaflet does boast of 'beautiful architecture' but it also shows pictures of buildings which look clean, modern and exciting. Its claim that it has 'a remarkable industrial heritage' refers to the same buildings which Orwell condemned as 'ugly'. Similarly, the impression of pollution which is mentioned so much by Orwell (the yellow river and the air filled with smoke) is contradicted by the leaflet. The pictures are important in showing that the city is not just green but also clean.

Your turn!

Now it's your turn to answer this type of question. Read the leaflet on Blackpool Zoo on the opposite page and the CAPS article that follows (on page 70). Then answer the question below.

Both of these texts are about zoos. Compare and contrast the impressions they give of zoos. (10)

Organise your answer into two paragraphs, using these headings:

- The article
- The leaflet.

Timing ▶▶

You should spend no more than 13–14 minutes on this question.

Tips

- Remember to look closely at 'what is said' in both texts.
- Use specific details from both texts.
- Remember the messages in the pictures.
- Notice this type of question takes a 'single focus' and asks you to organise your answer by text.
- It is good to establish the 'broad contrast', but you must look at the specific details in both texts.

Sad Eyes and Empty Lives

There are over 400 zoos in the UK today, ranging from small farm parks [...] to large safari parks and aquaria. Worldwide there are probably more than 10,000 zoos, with hundreds of thousands of animals held captive.

5 In the wild, animals react to their surroundings, avoiding predators, seeking food and interacting with others of their species – doing what they have evolved for. Consequently, even what might seem 'larger' or 'better' enclosures may be [...] impoverished in terms of the animals' real needs.

10 Frustration and boredom are commonplace amongst animals in zoos and can lead to obsessive and repetitive behaviours in the form of pacing, swaying, and even self-mutilation. This is known as stereotypic behaviour and such pointless, repetitive movements have also been noted in
15 people with mental illnesses. With nothing to do, animals in zoos go out of their minds. Disturbed maternal behaviour may involve over-grooming and the rejection or killing of young.

Even diets are unnatural, with zebras in zoos becoming
20 overweight as the grass they are given is higher in calories than the grasses of the African savannah. The resulting obesity can affect fertility.

Some animals suffer such serious behavioural problems in zoos that they are given anti-depressants, tranquillisers
25 and anti-psychotic drugs to control their behaviour.

A quarter of British zoos don't keep any threatened species and those that do only have them in very small numbers. Many animals are there just to draw in the tourists.

30 Many of the high-profile, co-ordinated breeding programmes amongst zoo bodies have no mechanism for returning animals to the wild. They simply provide for the continued breeding of certain species.

Zoos still take animals from the wild. Throughout the
35 1990s over 1,000 elephants were taken from the wild and sold to zoos and circuses and over 70% of elephants in European zoos were wild caught.

From *The Captive Animals' Protection Society*

Writing

Paper 2 Section B at a glance

You will have to produce two pieces of writing. The tasks set will be examples from the following:

- a letter (informal or formal)
- a report
- an article
- a leaflet
- a speech
- a review.

Advice

- The first writing task will probably be linked in some way to the reading material used in Section A of Paper 2.
- You have about 35 minutes to complete each question.
- You should aim to write between one and one-and-a-half sides in response to each question.
- Both questions will be marked out of 20.
- The examiners can give you up to 13 of the marks for what you write (i.e. content) and up to 7 marks for how you write (i.e. spelling, grammar and punctuation).
- Format (where appropriate), audience and purpose are important.

Transactional writing

Informal letters

- Read the question carefully and pay close attention to the audience specified.
- Set the letter out correctly.
- Plan your work carefully.
- Make sure that your tone is appropriate.
- Take care with spelling, grammar and punctuation.

How to set out an informal letter

The following is an example of how to set out an informal letter.

5 Broad Road
Lancaster ——— Your address
Lancashire
LA1 5GS

15th January 2009 ——— The date
Dear John, ——— Greeting (salutation)
This is the first paragraph of my letter. It is a short paragraph ——— Short introductory paragraph
that introduces my letter. It also introduces the purpose of ——— Purpose of the letter
the letter.

                                                              Three or four middle
-- paragraphs that cover the
                                                              points you wish to make
----

-- The letter will end with a
                                                              brief but important closing
This is the final paragraph of my letter. It is a short paragraph paragraph that will round off
but also an important one as it rounds off the purpose of the the purpose of the letter.
letter.
Love, ——— Informal closure
Amanda ——— Your first name

Sample question and answer

Read the task below, then read the sample student answer and examiner's comments that follow.

Sample question

Imagine you have a friend who has decided to run in the London Marathon (a distance of over 26 miles).

Write a letter to your friend or relative, giving your opinions. (20)

Sample answer

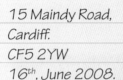

> 15 Maindy Road,
> Cardiff.
> CF5 2YW
> 16th, June 2008.
>
> Dear Hannah,
>
> I hope you had a good holiday. I know you needed a relaxing break but then I heard that the first thing you do on your return from Spain is to enter for the London marathon! Mind can't say I'm that surprised knowing you as I do.
>
> I know I could not talk you out of it, no matter how hard I tried. You're too stubborn. So I'm offering some advice so that you won't end up with any injuries that you always seem to get.
>
> Firstly I know you think that 26 miles will be no problem but you really should train. I don't mean just walking to the end of your garden and back. Eat fruit and vegetables. I know I sound like your Nan, but it really does give you more energy than crisps and chocolate. I would also suggest that you should drink water rather than those energy drinks. I want to say that I am very proud of you. It may not sound like I am but it is only that I am worried about you. I know you will reach your goal because you are so determined and I am sure you will be fine.
>
> Before you ask I will sponsor you. I think it is great you are showing such initiative and raising money for Save the Children. Good luck and keep up the good work.
>
> Love,
> Lilian.

Examiner's comments

This student has done what the question asked her to do. The letter is well set out and it is well organised. It has a pleasant tone – friendly, playful and concerned, and it is mostly accurate. This response was awarded a C grade.

How to improve this answer

There is clearly a lot that is right about this answer, though it could quite easily achieve higher marks if it:

- was a bit more ambitious
- included more detail
- was better organised
- built up the points a bit more
- said more about the actual event
- did a bit more to capture the tone of a friend writing to a friend.

Your turn!

Now it's your turn to attempt this type of task. Write a letter to a friend who has moved to another area to live, giving him/her news that he/she would be interested in. Remember to:

- set your letter out properly
- plan your paragraphs
- adopt the right tone
- take care with spelling, grammar and punctuation. **(20)**

Timing ▶▶

In the exam you should spend about 35 minutes on this task.

Tips

- Getting the tone right is very important for this sort of task. This task needs an informal tone.

- This task is marked out of 20. Of this, 13 marks are available for content (i.e. **what** you write), and 7 marks are available for grammar, spelling and punctuation (i.e. **how** you write). So, how you write is as important as what you write.

- You should aim to write between one and one-and-a-half sides.

Formal letters

Key revision points

In what ways will this be different from the informal letter we have just looked at?

- The layout – the address of the recipient will be included, the salutation (greeting) will be 'Dear named person', 'Dear Mr/Mrs/Miss', 'Dear Sir' or 'Dear Madam'. The ending will be 'Yours sincerely' if you know the name of the person you are writing to; it will be 'Yours faithfully' if you do not know their name. You should **not** use 'love' or 'best wishes' etc.
- The tone will be formal and business-like, **not** informal/friendly.

However, some of the things that are important in an informal letter will also be important here. These are:

- planning
- paragraphing
- technical accuracy.

Sample question and answer

Read the task below, then read the sample student answer and examiner's comments that follow.

Sample question

A local businessman has applied for permission to hold an outdoor music festival in your area.

Write a letter to your local newspaper either supporting or opposing this idea. **(20)**

Sample answer

On the following page is a student's answer. As you read it, think about the bullet points above. Where has he been successful and where could the work be improved? Some of the errors are highlighted in **bold**.

8 Astley Way,
Cowbridge.
CW10 4EU

'The Echo',
Marsh Street,
Cowbridge.
Dear Sir,

I am writing in **responce** to Mr. Palmer's letter **suggesting to hold** an outdoor music festival. I am writing to say I agree with the idea.

The first reason I agree is because I love music and it sounds like a fun idea it will also bring a lot of **intrest** to our area and may convince some people to move here.

The second is because lots of local businesses will benefit from this festival local shops that sell drink and food should do well and if Mr. Palmer uses a local catering firm they will benefit as well. So hopefully the festival will bring in lots of revenue for local businesses.

My third reason is that it will bring in people from all over. Some people would say that's a bad thing others that it **give's** the local people a chance to make new friends.

My **forth** and final reason is that this festival will highlight how good **are** area is at holding such events and would attract more festivals and concerts and may even gain an annual one which will create lots of revenue and boost **are areas and towns** economy.

To those who would say **its** going to be **to** loud or we will have drunks everywhere I would say no we won't because it's only at a few concerts that you get that and that if it is planned well there should be no trouble.

So to conclude I am for this festival mainly because I think it will raise **lot's** of revenue for businesses and open the door to an annual event.

Yours **sincerly**,
David Lloyd

Tip

Some of the errors have been highlighted in bold. Can you correct them and spot other errors?

Examiner's comments

The letter is quite well set out but there are errors, such as no date and the wrong closure. It is organised into paragraphs, is long enough and makes a decent case. This is a D grade response, but could easily be improved upon.

How to improve this answer

Improvements in spelling and punctuation, making the writing less awkward in places and getting rid of the repetition of some words and ideas, would help take this response up a grade or more. There are a number of errors, some of which have been highlighted in bold. These should not appear in an improved response.

Your turn!

Now it's your turn to attempt a formal letter. Re-write the student's formal letter opposite, making improvements as you go along. You could use the above suggestions on how to improve the answer to get you started.

Tips

Remember, marks are awarded for content (what you say) and for the way in which you write (the accuracy).

Reports

Key revision points

What is a report and what should it do?

- A report gives information so that the recipient has a better understanding of the subject that has been reported on.
- It will also advise and perhaps persuade and make recommendations. This should put the person or group of people for whom it is intended in a better position to take appropriate action.

As this is transactional writing, the following are very important.

- Format – it is vital that time is spent organising your work. Decide on an appropriate main heading and sub-headings for the subject you are asked to cover.
- Audience – make sure that you write for the audience. The question will clearly indicate who this is. It may be a head teacher, a school council, class members, a local authority, etc.
- Tone – this can vary quite a lot depending on the person(s) for whom the report is intended. It will sound different, for example, if you are writing for a head teacher rather than students of your own age.

 **Sample question and answer**

Read the question below, then read the sample student answer and examiner's comments that follow.

Sample question

Write a report for the governors of your school on the out-of-school activities available to the students. **(20)**

Sample answer

> I am issuing this report on out of school activities because of the trouble and kaos some children get up to. I know that the children are not your responsibility out of school hours but I thought you could do something to help for example holding a youth club once or twice a week. It doesn't have to be run by teachers and it could be a great way for the school to earn money for itself or other organisations. The school could also arrange other events such as discos or trips to places. Not only does this keep children off the streets it also gives them the opportunity to make new friends. Also there should be other school activities eg netball, football where all pupils are invited to watch.
>
> I am sure that you are all aware of the grafety and what some children get up to. That's why I'm sure you will be interested in my ideas. This scheme will do the community good and many people will be grateful to you. But mainly it will get the children off the streets and somewhere safe. This scheme could also decrease the crime level. Plus the school could benifit lots as well.
>
> I hope you take this report into consideration.

Examiner's comments

Generally, this report is accurately and clearly written though there are a few spelling mistakes, e.g. 'kaos' (chaos), 'grafety' (graffiti), 'benifit' (benefit). It is polite in tone and makes some sensible points. It was awarded a grade D.

How to improve this answer

This response could be improved in the following ways.

- The layout – it doesn't look like a report.
- The organisation of the points.
- The use of headings and paragraphs.
- An introduction explaining clearly what the report is about.
- A more effective conclusion.

Your turn!

Now it's your turn to work on a report.

Using the guidance above as a starting point, reorganise and develop the student's report on the opposite page. You will need to provide a main heading and then use the following sub-headings:

- **why the report is being presented**
- **the present situation**
- **facilities/activities that will improve the situation**
- **the benefits that will follow**
- **conclusion.**

You could now have a go at one or more of the following exam tasks.

1. Your school or college is concerned about the facilities for the disabled.

   Your head teacher or principal has asked you for a report outlining what has already been done to help the disabled, and suggesting improvements.

2. Your town or district has received a grant to improve local facilities.

   Write a report to the local council suggesting how this money could be spent to benefit the community.

3. Your school or college has decided to hold a 'Charity Fun Day'.

   The head teacher or principal has asked you to write a report to him/her suggesting which two charities you think should benefit, and why. Write your report.

Tip

If asked to complete a task such as this, base it on your experience of your own school/college. This will make your report sound more real and you should not be short of things to say.

◀◀ Timing

You have about 35 minutes to complete each task.

Articles for magazines and newspapers

Key revision points

- Articles tend to be written for newspapers and magazines. Their purpose is to inform and, in most cases, to entertain.
- Look carefully at the wording of the question.
- If help is given in the bullet points, don't be afraid to use some or all of it.
- Follow the instruction about the length of your answer.

 **CD-ROM**

Sample question and answer

Read the task below, then read the sample student answer and examiner's comments that follow.

Sample question

Filling about one to two pages in your answer book, write a lively article with the title 'The Joys of Exercise' for a magazine for people of your age.   (20)

Tips

- The key word in this task is 'lively'. But it is also vital to remember that writing accurately is really important.

- Note the audience, which will influence the way the article needs to be written.

Sample answer

The Joys of Exercise.

*Ever wondered what the point in it all is? You spend endless hours sweating pints, out of **breathe**, sick and **nautious** – and for what? A slightly slimmer figure; that's all!// I hate the thought of feeling as if someone was strangling my lungs, squeezing every last breath from my aching body. I feel dizzy at the thought of it all. And yet why do I do it, I hear you ask? Well, it's simply this: because the experts say so.// Surely it would make a little more sense to diet to shed those last few pounds instead? But no – we need to exercise to stay healthy. They say 30 minutes of exercise a day can help keep you in shape. If only it was as simple as that. Of course, they fail to mention that despite all this **excrutiating** exercise, we have to watch what we eat as well. Or rather what we don't eat –which by today's standards is pretty much everything! So again, I ask why do we do it? //Ok so fair enough maybe the evidence does say we should cause ourselves a heart attack or two exercising, in the name of keeping fit…but I wonder why we really put ourselves through such agony? I think **its** this. **Its** not for statistics. **Its** not to know that we should run half a mile without stopping, should we need to It's for our own self esteem. We feel proud to say we can swim that extra length. We're chuffed to be able to run up and down the stairs without losing our puff. And we can finally have that confidence to strip off into our bathers and not worry about what everyone else is thinking of us. // So this summer take it upon yourself to fitten up. Its may not be fun but it sure is fantastic to see the end result. Occupy yourself with something constructive this summer – get fit.*

> **Tip**
>
> Some of the errors have been highlighted in bold. Can you correct them and spot other errors?

Examiner's comments

It sounds like an article and is lively and interesting. There is a good sense of audience and there are some nice touches such as the use of questions to involve the reader and the use of exclamation marks to indicate the tone of voice. There are some informal touches such as 'fair enough' and 'we're chuffed'. It was awarded a grade B.

How to improve this answer

Organise it into paragraphs – perhaps five. Get rid of the spelling and punctuation errors in the student's response. As the examiner's comments above suggest, there is a lot that is right about this response. Spelling, punctuation and organisation problems are the things that would prevent this answer from being a grade A.

Your turn!

Now have a go at the following task:

1. A magazine is running a series of articles for parents under the title 'An Enjoyable Day Out for the Family'.

Write an article recommending a place to visit, and explaining its appeal to all the family. You might think about a town, a seaside resort, a theme park or a museum, but you are free to make your own choice. **(20)**

You could also have a go at one or more of the following:

2. **Write an article for a newspaper magazine entitled 'Teenage Trends'. You might like to think about trends in music, fashion, etc.**

3. **Write an article for a teenage magazine entitled 'Compulsory Sport in Schools'. Describe the present situation and then give your honest opinion of what is offered and whether big changes are needed.**

4. **Write an article for a newspaper or magazine under the title 'Young People Today'.**

5. **Write an article for a newspaper or magazine on a place that is well worth visiting.**

Tips

- Plan what you want to say.
- Organise your article into paragraphs.
- Think of your audience and how you should write for it.
- Make what you have to say interesting.
- Take care to write accurately.
- Be creative and distinctive – examiners like to be entertained!

Timing ▶▶

Aim to spend about 35 minutes on this task.

Leaflets

Key revision points

- A leaflet is a neat and effective way of giving information or of advertising, for example, an amenity. Its purpose is to inform, advise and persuade.
- If you are asked to write a leaflet in the examination you will get no credit for drawing pictures.
- You will need to show that you understand the purpose of a leaflet and are able to adapt your writing to suit the stated audience.
- You will also need to show that you are able to adopt the right tone and style.
- It is sufficient to show your understanding of format by using suitable headings and perhaps indicating where pictures/diagrams might be placed.

Sample question and answer

Read the task below, then read the sample student answer and examiner's comments that follow.

Sample question

Your school or college is running a campaign during its 'Healthy Eating' week to persuade students to buy and eat more fruit. It has asked you to produce a leaflet that will be given out in the dining hall.

Write your leaflet. (20)

Tip

Look out for leaflets when in shops, hotels, visitor attractions and other places. Study how they are presented and the methods they use to inform, advise and persuade.

Sample answer

Healthy Eating

Eating healthily doesn't have to be uncool.

This week a wide range of healthy foods, optional of course will be available to students.

Don't be preasured into not eating healthy foods by friends, think of all the people they look up to such as maybe a famous footballer or a netball player.

How do you think they keep in good shape?

Well my friend it's all down to their diet and exercise, eating fruit can give you the energy you need for a good workout and to keep you fit.

Spots can become a major problem during your school life and so can your size.

Eating fruit and vegetables is good for your skin and can help get rid of spots

For those of you lads in school during P.E. who are trying to tone up those muscles why stress when you can concentrate on a healthy diet giving you the energy you need for a good workout and gradually building up your muscles.

How do you think a physical trainer builds up their muscles and ends up looking like this.

Pictures of Physical trainer

Eating healthily isn't always for the uncool and the less popular people so think wisely about what you eat wether your friends like it or not.

83

Examiner's comments

In this response the student has used columns to make the work look like a leaflet and has also indicated where some illustrations are to be included. This is fine though you do not have to do this. The work has some good features such as:

- the focus on the task
- the organisation/shape
- the tone
- sense of audience
- the clarity.

So overall this was awarded a grade C.

How to improve this answer

Sub-headings could have been used and it could be more detailed (points could be developed). Sentence control could be better, for example at the end of the second paragraph, and the spelling is not always accurate, e.g. 'preasured'. With a bit more detail and ambition this could have got more than the C grade awarded.

Tips

- You may wish to indicate where you would use illustrations, but you will be rewarded for the quality of your writing, not your illustrations.

- Make sure the purpose of the leaflet is clear. In this instance it's to **persuade** students.

- Make sure the audience is clear. In this instance your fellow students.

- Follow any advice given about what the examiner expects you to do.

Timing ▶▶

You should spend about 35 minutes completing this task.

Your turn!

Below are some more leaflet questions. Try one or more of these, remembering that the following are some features of good leaflets:

- a heading that makes it clear what the leaflet is about
- sub-headings or sections so that the information can be easily located
- bullet points – these help to make it more attractive
- an appropriate tone
- a good sense of audience.

1. **You have been asked to produce a leaflet to persuade people in your area to be more careful about litter and waste. Write your leaflet. You may wish to indicate where you would use illustrations, but you will be rewarded for the quality of your writing, not your illustrations.** (20)

2. **Your school or college is concerned about its provision for the disabled. Your head teacher or principal has asked you for a report outlining what has already been done to help the disabled, and suggesting improvements.** (20)

3. **Your local junior school has invited you to produce a leaflet about the importance of a healthy lifestyle, aimed at ten- and eleven-year-olds. The leaflet should be informative and persuasive. Write your leaflet.** (20)

Writing a speech

Key revision points

- An exam question that asks you to write a speech will tell you the purpose of the speech and the audience to write for.
- The **purpose** is to inform, persuade, advise and to raise issues.
- The **audience** will vary. It could be for a specific age group or for a wide age range. The question will make this clear, though.
- The **tone** should be polite, though it will depend, to a certain extent, on who is being addressed.
- The features of a good speech are:
  - it will start by addressing the audience
  - it will make clear what the subject is and will be well organised
  - points will be made clearly
  - interesting information to back up a case will be carefully selected
  - care will be taken to hold the attention of the audience
  - there will be a strong conclusion and acknowledgement of the audience: 'Thank you for listening'.

Sample question and answer

Read the question below, then read the sample student answer and examiner's comments that follow. Note: not all of the student's answer is included – the missing sections are indicated with '…'.

Sample question

As part of your 'Speaking and Listening' activities you have to prepare a class talk. You have decided to talk about the use of mobile phones in schools. Write your talk. **(20)**

> **Tip**
>
> In the exam you may be asked to write the script of a speech/talk or the question could ask you to make an extended contribution to a radio phone-in. In both, you will be giving your views and trying to argue/inform/persuade.

Sample answer

Fellow pupils, I have chosen as the topic of my talk today a subject we seem to read and hear a lot about. Mobile phones.

These have been around now for a long time but still the argument goes on whether or not we should be allowed to bring our phones to school. As with most things there are points for and against.

I will start with the downside. Teachers say that they distract us from our work. They say that we are more interested in text messages than we are in our school texts and preparing for our G.CS.E.'s. They also say that it is not acceptable to have phones go off in the middle of the lesson. Well, I disagree with the first but agree with the second. It's not fair to say that they stop us working but obviously we can't have a situation where ring tones are interrupting the teaching. There is, though, an easy solution – all phones to be switched off during lesson time (and that includes the teacher's phones). Another point made is that mobiles can be used to help students cheat in exams. . . .

Yes there are issues but there are also a lot of real advantages. If our parents want to contact us urgently then they can do so. This has happened to me and I don't know what I would have done without my mobile. . . .

To sum up I think as I know most of you do that mobiles have more good points than bad ones. Yes they are abused by the odd person here and there but most of us use them responsibly. We can't go on living in the past. We have to use modern technology to our advantage. If we don't then just look at what happened to the dinosaurs.

Thank you very much for listening.

Examiner's comments

This is a good piece of work which would have achieved a high grade, i.e. A/A*. It is on task and there is a strong sense of audience and purpose (i.e. to persuade). Persuasive techniques such as repetition are used and it is clearly argued. The organisation is good and it is accurately written.

Your turn!

Choose one of the following topics and write your own speech.

1. A radio phone-in programme is dealing with the subject of smoking and, in particular, smoking in public places. You have decided to contribute and have decided to write down what you intend to say before you are asked for your view. Write what you would say. (20)

2. Your debating society in school intends to discuss the subject of boxing. You have been asked to contribute. The audience will be fellow students. Write what you would say. (20)

3. You have been asked to prepare a talk/speech to be presented to your class on a subject of your choice. Write what you would say. (20)

Timing

You should spend about 35 minutes on the task.

Tips

To make your speech interesting/effective:

- adopt an appropriate tone
- use rhetorical devices such as 'I'm sure you will agree', 'It is often claimed that…'
- use humour if appropriate
- use statistics, but sparingly
- use personal experience
- don't be afraid to be controversial.

Reviews

Key revision points

- A review is a critical opinion of a book, film, a piece of music or CD, a television programme, play, etc.
- It needs a suitable heading, usually the name of the film, or the name of the book and its author, or the name of the CD and the performer and so on.
- The structure will include an introduction followed by paragraphs that will discuss the book, CD, etc.
- Finally, there will be an overall opinion and recommendation.
- A star rating may also be included.
- The audience can be a specific one, e.g. young people, or the public generally, i.e. anyone who might be interested in the film, book, etc.

 **CD-ROM**

Sample question and answer

Read the question below, then read the sample student answer and examiner's comments that follow.

Sample question

Write a review of a book, film or music CD for a magazine which is read by people of your age. **(20)**

Your review should include:

- details about the book, film or CD you have chosen
- comments on its strengths, if any
- comments on its weaknesses, if any
- a clear recommendation.

Sample music review answer

TLC's 3D

The R'N'B multi platinum trio girl group have released their final album as tribute to the lost group member Lisa Lopes who died in a car accident last year. The album contains a wide range of music styles such as; R'N'B , hip-hop ,reggae, rap and even blues. TLC hope to blow up the charts with newly released tracks 'Girl Talk', 'Hands Up' and 'Quickie'.

The album has many strengths with many power ballad and soulfull tracks making it a must have album. The tracks are all different with different messages about life which is important to youths of today. Even with the loss of a member the album still packs some great beats and lyrics.

However, the death of Lisa has effected the album on its rap content because she was the main rapper so the album contains hardly no rap which is a downfall as TLC albums were known for the hard core rap in their songs.

Overall the album is great, worth the money and finalizes a decade of music by one of the world's greatest female groups. And what a way they went out, despite the damage to them they got back on their feet and left a mark on the music industry. TLC 3D out now in most record stores. Buy now before they get sold out.

Examiner's comments

This student clearly knows what a music review looks like and sounds like. It is well organised and he has made good use of the bullet points suggested by the question. There is a good sense of the intended audience and there are effective touches such as 'must-have album' and 'packs some great beats and lyrics'. This was awarded a strong C grade.

How to improve this answer

To improve this answer, it would help to focus on the slips and errors with spelling, punctuation (such as the use of commas where there should be full stops) and paragraphing (the second-to-last paragraph is clumsily written).

Your turn!

First you could correct the errors and tidy up the second-to-last paragraph. Then:

1. **Write your own music review.**   **(20)**

You could also have a go at one or more of the following. You will find examples of film and book reviews, written by students, on the CD-ROM.

2. **Write a review of either a film you really enjoyed, or one you really disliked, for teenage readers. Base your work on a film you have actually seen!**   **(20)**

3. **Write a review of a book you have read recently. Your review is intended for a teenage magazine. This may be a book that you enjoyed, one you disliked, or one you have mixed feelings about.**   **(20)**

Tip

For Task 1, choose music that really interests you and that you know something about. You will be tested not on your musical taste but on your ability to put together an effective review.

Chapter 5

Prose

The set novel

Prose extract questions

- The extract question is intended to test your close reading skills.
- First, check the focus of the question(s), then highlight or underline key words and phrases throughout the extract that will help you in your answer. Look particularly closely at the beginning and ending.
- In your answer, make sure you put the extract in context – that you show you know how it fits into the novel as a whole.
- Make your point of view clear straight away and be specific. For example, if the question is about mood and atmosphere, say straightaway what you think the mood and atmosphere are.
- Back up your points with evidence from the text.
- Then tackle the key areas of the extract, selecting detail as you go. Start from the content – what is actually going on in the extract – then show how the parts you've decided to select are significant. **Don't forget the question!**

Sample question and answer – Higher Tier

Read the sample student response and the examiner's comments after the answer.

The extract, which you will find on the CD-ROM, is from *To Kill a Mockingbird*. In the extract, three children are playing. The older brother, Jem, tries to scare his little sister, Scout and their friend, Dill with ghost stories of 'Hot Steams'. Annoyed at not getting the reaction he wanted, he pushes Scout, who is in a tyre, extra hard, and she ends up close to the house of the Radley family, of whom the whole community, and particularly the children, are scared.

CD-ROM

Sample question

With close reference to the extract, show how Harper Lee creates mood and atmosphere here. **(10)**

Sample answer (extract)

Harper Lee creates mood and atmosphere by using emotive language to describe what's happening. She uses short sentences and lots of punctuation which makes the reader read it fast and pick up on the urgency she wants you to feel. She makes you start to panic for the children. At the beginning of the extract she makes the children exaggerate a lot. They use emotive language 'wallows around','wrapping around you'.

Too general – what type of mood and atmosphere?

Very general, and no support/examples given.

Awareness of mood and atmosphere.

Simple statement out of context, and general.

Simple spotting of words. How are these emotive?

Examiner's comments

This extract from a response is not considering the context of Harper Lee's extract, and is operating at D/E level.

How to improve this answer

To get to grade C or above, it needs to look at the extract in the context of what is happening, and to select and highlight specific details – in other words, to pick out words and phrases and show how they work in that particular extract. You will find an additional sample answer on the CD-ROM.

Your turn!

The following task will help you start a 'mood and atmosphere' extract answer. Choose a short extract from your set novel which you think creates mood and atmosphere. You could ask your teacher to help you choose a suitable extract. Then write the opening paragraph of your response in answer to the following task.

**With close reference to the extract, show how ....
creates mood and atmosphere here.** **(10)**

Tips

- Make sure you say something specific about the mood and atmosphere.

- Select and highlight detail to support your overview (main point).

◄◄ Timing

Remember that you only have 20 minutes in the exam, including reading and thinking time, so keep an eye on the clock as you do the task.

Exam prose extract questions – Higher Tier

You might like to practise some or all of the following questions. They are typical of the questions you are likely to see in your exam.

1. With close reference to the extract, show how …. creates mood and atmosphere here.

2. Look closely at how …. speaks and behaves here. What does it reveal about his/her state of mind?

3. Look closely at how …. speaks and behaves here. How does it affect your feelings towards him/her?

4. How does …. suggest ….'s feelings in this extract?

Sample question and answer – Foundation Tier

On the Foundation Tier, you may be asked to give your thoughts and feelings about the extract. Read the following sample student response, together with the examiner's comments about the answer.

The extract, which you will find on the CD-ROM, is from *Of Mice and Men.* In the extract, Lennie is killed by George. Lennie had just accidentally killed a woman (Curley's wife) on the ranch where he has been working with his close friend, George. George kills Lennie to spare him being tortured by the other ranch workers. As you read the responses, think about which one is likely to get the best mark, and why.

Sample questions

(i) **What are your thoughts and feelings as you read this extract?**

(ii) **Choose parts of this extract that you find effective. Write about them, explaining why you find them effective.**

Sample answer

(i) As I read this extract my thoughts are shocked as it is so — *Aware/personal response*
unexpected, I thought that George was going to take Lennie
to another place and they'd try to get a job someplace else. — *Engaged/aware of context*
My feelings as I read this extract were also shocked and it
was a very sad ending for such a good book, what made me
sad was thinking about George and Lennie owning their own
house and now it's all gone. — *Simple empathy*

(ii) 'Le's do it now. Le's get that place now' Lennie begged. That
extract was very sad because he had been wanting to go
into their own house for ages and now he gets very excited
because he thinks that him and George are going on the run
again, but George knows that it has got to end there. — *Selects and comments*

Examiner's comments

There are very good qualities in this answer: the student has
understood the context, and responded to the extract with
awareness and engagement, but just hasn't written enough, and
because the answer doesn't highlight detail, it would get D/E.

How to improve this answer

This answer could have achieved Grade C if the student had
tracked through the extract, focusing more on specific words
and phrases. You will find another sample response on the
CD-ROM.

Your turn!

The following will help you with a 'thoughts and feelings' extract question. Choose an extract from your set novel that creates strong thoughts and feelings. You could ask your teacher to help you choose a suitable extract. Then have a go at writing about it in two parts:

(i)   **What are your thoughts and feelings as you read the extract?**

(ii) **Select words and phrases that you find effective and write about them, explaining why you find them effective.**

Exam prose extract questions – Foundation Tier

You might like to practise some or all of the following questions. They are typical of the questions you are likely to see in your exam.

1. (i)   What are your thoughts and feelings as you read this extract?
   (ii) Choose parts of the extract that you find effective. Write about them, explaining why you find them effective.

2. (i)   What do you think of the way .... speaks and behaves here? Give reasons for what you say.
   (ii) What do you think of the way .... speaks and behaves here? Give reasons for what you say.

3. (i)   What are your thoughts and feelings about .... here? Give reasons for what you say.
   (ii) What are your thoughts and feelings about .... here? Give reasons for what you say.

4. (i)   What does this extract show you about ....'s feelings?
   (ii) Choose parts of this extract that you find effective and write about them, explaining why you find them effective.

Prose essay questions – Higher Tier

Character questions

Key revision points

You need to be clear about the main characters.

- Make notes on each main character's journey through the novel.
- Note particularly the first and last time you see them, and what we learn about them then.
- Include notes on their relationships with other characters and how and why they change.
- Select a few key quotations (just a word or two may well be enough) that you think represent the character well.

Sample question and answer

Read the opening from a sample response on the following page, together with the examiner's comments about it. The response is based on the novel *Paddy Clarke Ha Ha Ha* by Roddy Doyle, which is told from the point of view of a ten-year-old boy growing up in Ireland in the 1960s. During the novel, Paddy's parents separate.

Sample question

Imagine you are Paddy's mother. At the end of the novel you think back over its events. Write down your thoughts and feelings. Remember how Paddy's mother would speak when you write your answer. (20)

Sample answer (opening)

I can't stop thinking about the poor children. When Patrick shook his father's hand, it was like an innocent, scared little boy, shaking hands with a scary, unpredictable stranger. Mind, I don't blame my Patrick at all for his reaction. After him witnessing his father hit me in the kitchen, I don't know how he could see him in the same light again. He is no role model for his son. I'm so terribly distraught that Paddy had to witness the event and wish that he hadn't. I think that is the main reason his father left. There is no justified reason why a man should hit his wife; nothing can compensate for what he did, and I think dear Patrick is aware of that, God bless him.

Strong sense of Paddy's mother's voice immediately.

Specific reference to the ending of the novel.

Discussion of characters and relationships – and she *would* call Paddy Patrick!

Specific highlighting of important detail.

Sensitive understanding of characters and relationships.

Tips

- Aim to 'sound like' the character.
- Include references to their relationships with other characters.
- Select and highlight some key moments from the novel.

Examiner's comments

This is a very strong opening to an empathy response. There's a clear voice, sensitivity to characters and relationships, and references to important times in the novel (including its ending). Already this is showing signs of A/A* potential.

Your turn!

Choose one of the main characters from your set novel. Then write the opening paragraph to an empathy response from the point of view of that character.

Theme questions

Key revision points

- Jot down what you think are the main themes in your set novel.
- For each theme, make notes on how the themes are shown through what happens in the novel.
- Link the themes to each main character.
- Choose four or five short quotations for each theme.

Your turn!

Choose one of the key themes from your set novel. Then write the opening paragraph to one of the following questions.

1. How does .... present the theme of .... in ....?

2. How important is the theme of .... in ....?

- Aim to start with a strong opening sentence. Sometimes a well chosen quotation can be very effective.

- Refer to the question (i.e. to the theme you are writing about) as soon as possible.

- Make sure you include direct references to the text in this opening paragraph.

Title questions

Key revision points

- With this sort of open question you can't go wrong if you support what you say with details from the text.
- Remember that the titles of some novels, such as *Of Mice and Men*, have a special significance.
- Write down the title of your set text, then brainstorm ideas relating to the title – think of things to do with characters, things to do with themes, and things to do with the plot (what happens).

Sample question and answer

Read the following extract from a sample response, together with the examiner comments around it. It is based on *I Know Why The Caged Bird Sings*, in which Maya Angelou tells the story of her early life in the American Deep South in the early twentieth century.

Sample question

To what extent do you find *I Know Why The Caged Bird Sings* an effective title for Maya Angelou's account of her childhood?

Sample answer (extract)

...Later, in her childhood, she spends a month at the junkyard with other children. These children are clearly caged by their misfortune and homelessness. However, the group work like an organisation and survive admirably due to their circumstances. Even Maya gains invaluable experience – 'It set a tone of tolerance in my life.' She experiences total acceptance with a group of mixed race children and this brings hope and general optimism to her. The bird carries on singing... .

Reference to key episode in the book.

Reference to the title/ question.

Direct reference to the text.

Overview and evaluation.

Reference to title/question/ symbolism.

Tips

- Make sure you include coverage of key areas of the whole text.
- Include references to the themes of the novel.
- Include relevant discussion of characters and relationships.

Examiner's comments

This is an extract from a much longer response, but it already reveals many high-grade qualities, such as assured reference to key aspects of the text, evaluation of characters and relationships, and appreciation of stylistic features, with the symbolism of the caged bird. These are A/A* indicators.

Your turn!

Plan your response to a question on the significance of the title of your set novel.

Questions focusing on specific incidents and their importance

Key revision points

- Make a note of five or six key parts of the text, making sure you cover the whole text, from beginning to end.
- For each part you select, jot down some ideas about its importance – what it shows about characters, their development, and relationships with others, how it fits into the novel as a whole, and any themes it may highlight.
- Choose a few key, short quotations for each part you have chosen.

Now that you have read the key revision points, you could have a go at one or more of the sample essay questions that follow on page 99.

Exam prose essay questions – Higher Tier

You might like to practise some or all of the following questions. They are typical of the questions you are likely to see in your exam.

Character questions

1. Write about the relationship between .... and .... and how it is presented.

2. What do you think of .... and the way s/he is presented to the reader?

3. Imagine you are .... . At the end of the novel, you think back over its events. Write down your thoughts and feelings. Remember how .... would speak when you write your answer.

4. In your opinion, who or what had the greatest influence on ....? Support your answer with detailed reference to the text.

5. To what extent is it possible to feel sympathy for ....? Support your answer with detailed reference to the text.

6. How is the character of .... important to the novel as a whole?

7. Show how and why the character of .... changes throughout the novel.

Tip

There is always at least one question on character or characters on each prose text.

◀◀ **Timing**

In the exam you should spend about 40 minutes on this question (including thinking time).

Theme questions

1. How does .... present the theme of .... in ....?

2. How important is the theme of .... in ....?

Title questions

1. Why do you think .... called the novel ....?

2. To what extent do you find .... an effective title for the novel?

Questions focusing on specific incidents and their importance

How is .... important to the novel as whole?

Prose essay questions – Foundation Tier

Character questions

Sample question and answer

Read the following sample response, together with the examiner comments around it. It is based on a question on the novel *Stone Cold* by Robert Swindells, which is about homeless young people in London being targeted by a psychopath called Shelter.

Sample question

Write about the character of Ginger. Explain his importance to the novel as a whole.

Think about:

- the friendship between Link and Ginger
- the effect that Ginger's disappearance has on Link
- the importance of Ginger to the novel as a whole.

Sample answer

Ginger is a very important character in Stone Cold because he shows Link the ropes. Not only does he help Link he becomes Link's friend. Robert Swindells created a character to help Link survive not just through homelessness but mentally. Swindells did this by first showing Ginger as harmless, 'Is this your doorway? Sorry I'll move.' This shows Link's scared and doesn't want to get into trouble but Ginger replies 'No, it's alright just budge over a bit.' Because Ginger was nicer than most homeless people Link tried to become Ginger's friend and succeeded. At first Ginger is not that important but as the novel progresses Link and Ginger become very close friends.

Ginger is Link's teacher, 'here watch this'. If Ginger was not in the novel then Link's knowledge of homelessness would not be the same as he started clueless and perhaps Link would not have survived.

Although Ginger is 'streetwise' that doesn't stop Shelter from killing him. Swindells showed that this very much affected Link by Link searching for Ginger, 'Have you seen Ginger lately?' Swindells made Link break down slightly, 'I keep seeing a shadow, the shadow of Ginger, leaving me.'

Swindells also made Ginger important because if Ginger had not gone missing Shelter would not have been caught at the time he was. Also when Link is in Shelter's house and sees Ginger under the floor boards he fights with every strength he has. Ginger although dead was the reason Shelter was caught, this shows how important he is in the novel because every reader wants Shelter to be caught and wants Link safe. Ginger did both.

Clear focus on the question from the beginning.

Overview.

Good focus on specific detail from early in the novel.

Discussing characters and relationships.

Clear focus on the second part of the question.

Well-selected detail to support point made, addressing the second bullet point in the question.

Clear overview and understanding of the importance of Ginger's character.

Strong conclusion.

Examiner's comments

This is a well-focused response to the question. It does not just tell the story, but selects key points from the whole of the novel. Points made are supported by references to the text. The understanding of the importance of the character of Ginger to the novel as a whole is what makes this a secure grade C.

Tips

- Think about the first and last time you see your chosen character and what that tells you about him or her.

- Select key points in the story that are important to your chosen character's part in the novel.

- Make sure you show your understanding of how your chosen character is important to the novel as a whole.

Tips

- If you are given bullet points, be sure to use them to organise your answer.

- You should aim to write at least one paragraph for each bullet point.

- Remember that you can always add your own ideas too!

Your turn!

Choose one of the main characters from your set novel. Plan your answer to a question on your thoughts on that character, and his or her importance to the novel as a whole.

Exam prose essay questions – Foundation Tier

These questions will be more simply expressed than those on the Higher Tier, or will be more likely to have bullet points to help you in your answer, as follows.

1. What do you think of ....? [may be followed by bullet points to help you].

2. Write about .... [may be followed by bullet points to help you].

3. Imagine you are .... . At the end of the novel you think back over its events. Write down your thoughts and feelings [may be followed by bullet points to help you].

Chapter 6

Drama

The set play

Drama extract questions – Higher Tier

Sample question and answer

Read the following section taken from a sample student response, together with the examiner's comments on the answer.

The extract, which you will find on the CD-ROM, is from *Blood Brothers*. In the extract, Mrs Lyons, who is unable to have children, has persuaded her cleaner, Mrs Johnstone, to let her have one of the twins she is expecting but is now forbidding her from seeing her son, by giving her the sack and threatening her.

Sample question

Read the extract, then answer the following question.

Look closely at how Mrs Lyons speaks and behaves here. What does it reveal to an audience about her? (10)

Sample answer (extract)

Mrs. Lyons is presented as a selfish back stabber in this extract. This is because she wants everything to go her way, which is reflected when she lies to her husband, "I've got lots of things to buy." At this point we get the impression that she does not care about anything else but what she wants, which makes her seem selfish. Mrs Lyons is also going back on her word when she said that Mrs Johnstone could come and see the baby whenever she likes.

In this extract she also comes forward as rather controlling. There is a lot of imperative statement in this extract such as "sit down" when she is talking to Mrs. Johnstone, and this goes to show her character as very imperative.

Strong judgement to open – 'setting out stall'.

Judgement supported by reference to the text.

Aware of the context.

Clear judgement.

Spotting stylistic features, with limited exploration of their effect.

Examiner's comments

There are positive qualities to this extract from the student's response, and it makes clear what the student's point of view of the character is. However, there is 'empty spotting' in the second paragraph and this makes the answer a clear grade C, while the opening paragraph had the potential for a higher grade.

How to improve this answer

The response needs to be more systematic, with points made, supported and developed. Closer focus on the effects of how it is written would be useful, too. You will find an additional sample answer on the CD-ROM.

Tips

- Make clear points about the character.
- Look closely at the dialogue (speech) in the extract.
- Look closely at how characters interact with one another.
- Read the stage directions as closely as you do the dialogue.

Timing

Remember you only have 20 minutes in the exam, including reading and thinking time, so keep an eye on the clock as you do the task.

Your turn!

The following task will help you start a drama character extract answer. Choose an extract from your set text which you think presents a character in an interesting way. You could ask your teacher to help you choose a suitable one; then, write the opening paragraph of your response in answer to the question:

Look closely at how .... speaks and behaves here. What does it reveal to an audience about him/her?

Exam drama extract questions

You might like to practise some or all of the following questions. They are typical of the questions you are likely to see in your exam.

1. Look closely at how .... speaks and behaves here. What impressions would an audience receive of his/her character?

2. Look closely at how .... speaks and behaves here. How might it affect an audience's feelings towards him/her?

> **Tip**
>
> Typical extract questions on the Higher Tier for the drama text are similar to those for the prose text (page 92), but also include ones specific to a play.

Drama extract questions – Foundation Tier

Sample question and answer

Read the following section from a sample student response (on page 106) together with the examiner's comments on the answers.

The extract, which you will find on the CD-ROM, is from *A View from the Bridge*. It is set in Brooklyn, New York, in the 1950s. Two illegal immigrants, Marco and Rodolfo, have just arrived at the home of their relatives, Eddie and Beatrice Carbone, and their adopted niece, Catherine.

A scene from the production of *A View from the Bridge*, 1958

Sample questions

(i) What do you think of the way Eddie speaks and behaves here? Give reasons for what you say.

(ii) How do you think an audience would respond to this part of the play? Give reasons for what you say.

Sample answers

(i) Eddie speaks quite aggressive and annoyed 'Hey, kid – hey, wait a minute' as he interrupts Rodolfo from singing he is being rude. He also shows jealousy as no one else sings and Rodolfo has just arrived. He is jealous and Catherine enjoys his singing he is becoming popular already and Eddie may be afraid that he is going to be just left and not be the man of the house any more. Eddie is behaving in a different manner and he is being protective. He is wanting things to calm down. I think that he is becoming too wary and should step down.

Awareness of tone.

Subtext – reading between the lines.

Empathy and speculation ('may be…') as well as aware of wider context.

Engaged personal response.

(ii) The audience would respond to this part in the play by watching carefully as it is quite tense. They will be wanting to know what is going to happen. They may also be angry at Eddie for his behaviour towards Rodolfo. I think that the audience will be wanting Rodolfo and Marco to make a good impression on Eddie and to become more involved in things.

Aware of mood and atmosphere.

General but engaged personal response.

Examiner's comments

There are positive qualities to this answer: empathy and awareness and some discussion of characters. However, the student has not read closely enough, or written in enough detail, particularly in part (ii). This answer is a good D.

How to improve this answer

More careful tracking through the extract, with closer reading of the stage directions and more specific reference to the extract, in part (ii) in particular, would have got this answer to a clear grade C. You will find an additional sample response on the CD-ROM.

Your turn!

The following will help you with an 'effect on audience' extract question. Choose an extract from your set play that you think would have an impact on an audience. You could ask your teacher to help you choose a suitable extract. Then have a go at writing about it in two parts, as follows.

(i) **What do you think of the way .... speaks and behaves here? Give reasons for what you say.**

(ii) **How do you think an audience would respond to this part of the play? Give reasons for what you say.**

◀◀ Timing

Remember you only have 20 minutes in the exam, including reading and thinking time, so keep an eye on the clock as you do the task.

Tips

- Select fairly short extracts from your set play (around a page is ideal).

- Decide on a focus – characters or mood and atmosphere.

- Highlight key words and phrases – make sure you cover the whole of the extract, including its ending.

- Pay as much attention to the stage directions as to the dialogue.

- Make notes on how the details you have highlighted support your overview (your 'take' on the question focus).

- Make sure you write in detail, and focus on words and details from the extract. This is what will get you a Grade C or above in the exam.

Exam drama extract questions

You might like to practise the following questions; they are typical of the questions you are likely to see in the exam.

1. What do you think of the way .... speaks and behaves here?

2. How do you think an audience would respond to this part of the play?

Tip

Typical extract questions on the Foundation Tier for the drama text are also similar to those for the prose text (page 94), but include ones specific to a play.

Drama essay questions

Drama essay questions at a glance

On both Higher and Foundation Tiers the patterns for drama essay questions are similar to those for the essay questions on the prose set text in Section A of the exam paper (see pages 99 and 102), but there is one type of essay specific to the drama section:

Give advice to the actor playing .... on how she or he should present the character to an audience.

When this question is set on the Foundation Tier it may well have bullet points, too ('Think about...'). Remember to aim to write at least one paragraph for each bullet point.

Key revision points

- Remember that you are giving the actor in the question your opinions on the character he or she is playing.
- There is no need to give your ideas for staging the play, or costumes and make-up.
- You should give your opinions on how the character would be expected to speak and behave at important points in the play.
- Explain your points clearly, and include detailed reference to the text (it may help to imagine that the actor doesn't know the play very well!).

Advice to actor questions

Sample question and answer

Read the following student answer together with the examiner's comments about the answer. Play the CD-ROM to see examples of different questions and sample answers at different levels.

Sample question

Give advice to an actor playing Marco, one of the illegal immigrants in *A View from the Bridge*, on how he should present the character to an audience.

Sample answer (extract)

....Now the last scene I'll give you advice on is the scene where the immigration police come and take you away. Now it is really important in this scene that you show rage in your actions and voice, just think about how this scumbag Eddie can betray you and your family – it's a dishonour. So when you run in and spit in his face show the most aggression you can. And also scream that he killed your children Let the whole world know that the traitor killed your family.

— Reference to the text.

— Aware of mood/character.

— Reference to characters and relationships.

— Cultural context.

— Direct reference to the text.

— Subtext/cultural context.

Examiner's comments

This extract from the student's answer is a very lively response and includes close reference to some of the events of the play, and an understanding of the social and cultural background of the play. It is a clear grade C.

Your turn!

Choose one of the main characters in your set play, then plan your response to an 'advice to the actor' question.

Timing

In the exam you should spend about 40 minutes on the drama essay, including any thinking and planning time, so you need to get a move on!

Tips

- Focus on key points of the play (a maximum of five).

- Show an understanding of why your chosen character is behaving in specific ways.

- Discuss their relationships with other characters.

- Include references to the themes of the play.

- If you can, show an understanding of the playwright's use of language.

Chapter 7

Poetry

The unseen poem

The unseen poem at a glance

Although it's not very likely that you will have read the poem before, you will have seen the question on it and the bullet points before, as they are always the same.

Write about the poem and its effect on you

You may wish to include some or all of these points:

- the poem's content – what it is about
- the ideas the poet may have wanted us to think about
- the mood or atmosphere of the poem
- how it is written – words or phrases you find interesting, the way the poem is structured or organised, and so on
- your response to the poem.

Key revision points

- Take time to read the poem a few times before you start to write – you may change your mind from your first impressions. Also consider the title.
- Have a quick check to see if any of the words have been explained (with an asterisk '*' at the end of the poem) or if there are any notes to give you a lead in.
- As you read, underline key words and phrases, and annotate the poem.
- Use the same technique as with the extracts – decide on an overview (your 'take' on the poem), then see how your selected details fit into that overview.
- Start at the most obvious reading – there won't be any hidden tricks or traps!
- It's good to use words like 'perhaps' and 'maybe' – there isn't a 'right answer' and you'll get credit for your ideas, as long as they're supported by references to the poem.
- Comment on style (how it's written) but don't worry about using technical terminology – you can get just as good marks by looking at the words used, and don't get any extra marks for spotting techniques (in fact, that can get in the way of showing your understanding).
- Use the bullet points, but you don't need to write an equal amount on each one, and you can use them in any order.

Sample question and answer – Higher Tier

Read the following exam task, then read the sample student response together with the examiner's comments about the answer. The answer is in response to the poem 'A London Thoroughfare 2 A.M.', which follows. You will also find an additional sample answer on the CD-ROM.

Sample question

Write about the poem and its effect on you.

You may wish to include some or all of these points:

- the poem's content – what it is about
- the ideas the poet may have wanted us to think about
- the mood or atmosphere of the poem
- how it is written – words or phrases you find interesting, the way the poem is structured or organised, and so on
- your response to the poem.

A London Thoroughfare. 2 A.M.

They have watered the street,
It shines in the glare of lamps,
Cold, white lamps,
And lies
5 Like a slow-moving river,
Barred with silver and black.
Cabs go down it,
One,
And then another.
10 Between them I hear the shuffling of feet.
Tramps doze on the window-ledges,
Night-walkers pass along the sidewalks.
The city is squalid and sinister,
With the silver-barred street in the midst,
15 Slow-moving,
A river leading nowhere.

Opposite my window,
The moon cuts,
Clear and round,
20 Through the plum-coloured night.
She cannot light the city;
It is too bright.
It has white lamps,
And glitters coldly.

25 I stand in the window and watch the moon.
She is thin and lustreless,
But I love her.
I know the moon,
And this is an alien city.

Amy Lowell

Sample answer (opening paragraphs)

The title of Lowell's poem, 'A London Thoroughfare Two A.M.', immediately places both the setting and the time of day. The fact that it is at night reveals that the city would be in darkness, giving the poem an uncertain mood as it is unknown if the darkness will be inviting or hostile.

The poem is a reflection of the speaker's impressions of the city of London. The speaker is obviously new to the area as he/she describes it as 'an alien city', suggesting that he/she knows limited information about both the inhabitants and environment. The fact that he/she is a visitor is also suggested by the use of the word 'sidewalks' as a speaker from London would call them pavements.

The presence of light is a recurring theme throughout the poem, with repeated descriptions of the 'lamps' and 'moon'. However the 'lamps' seems clinical and unfriendly as the poet uses words such as 'cold' and describes the beam is a 'glare'. 'White' is the colour used to describe them, creating a sense of harsh spotlights.

Strong opening – immediately probing and speculating.

Using selected detail to read between the lines and make valid speculations.

Close focus on language choices and their effects.

Examiner's comments

This opening to a response works with the selected detail, building up an overview by exploring how the selected words and detail may fit into the overall picture. It already shows signs of grade A/A*.

Tips

- Be sure to use the bullet points.
- Don't forget to use the title to help you understand what the poem is about.
- Select and highlight detail to support your overview (main point).

Timing ▶▶

Remember you only have 30 minutes in the exam! Take about 10 minutes for thinking and note-making before you start writing.

Your turn!

Read the following poem carefully, jotting down notes and underlining key words and phrases as you do so; then complete the task.

Write about the poem and its effect on you.

You may wish to include some or all of these points:

- the poem's content – what it is about
- the ideas the poet may have wanted us to think about
- the mood or atmosphere of the poem
- how it is written – words or phrases you find interesting, the way the poem is structured or organised, and so on
- your response to the poem.

Stars and Planets

Trees are cages for them: water holds its breath
To balance them without smudging on its delicate
meniscus*.
Children watch them playing in their heavenly playground;
5   Men use them to lug ships across oceans, through firths*.

They seem so twinkle-still, but they never cease
Inventing new spaces and huge explosions
And migrating in mathematical tribes over
The steppes of space at their outrageous ease.

10   It's hard to think that the earth is one –
This poor sad bearer of wars and disasters
Rolls-Roycing round the sun with its load of gangsters,
Attended only by the loveless moon.

Norman MacCaig

*meniscus – surface
*firths – seas

 **Sample question and answer – Foundation Tier**

Read the following sample question, then read the extract from a sample student response together with the examiner's comments about the answer. The answer is in response to the poem entitled *Autumn*, which follows. You will also find an additional sample answer on the CD-ROM.

Sample question

Write about the poem and its effect on you.

You may wish to include some or all of these points:

- the poem's content – what it is about
- the ideas the poet may have wanted us to think about
- the mood or atmosphere of the poem
- how it is written – words or phrases you find interesting, the way the poem is structured or organised, and so on
- your response to the poem.

Autumn

Autumn arrives
Like an experienced robber
Grabbing the green stuff
Then cunningly covering his tracks
5   With a deep multitude
Of colourful distractions.
And the wind,
The wind is his accomplice
Putting an air of chaos
10 Into the careful diversions
So branches shake
And dead leaves are suddenly blown
In the faces of inquisitive strangers.
The theft chills the world
15 Changes the temper of the earth
Till the normally placid sky
Glows red with a quiet rage.

Alan Bold

Sample answer (extract)

The poem is about how Autumn steals away the summer and the warm months and replaces them with bare branches and colourful leaves on the ground. The strong wind is also part of Autumn 'putting on an air of chaos' by shaking the branches and making the leaves fall to the ground, but the dead leaves are suddenly blown and the naked branches and the cold wind 'chills the world' and fills the earth with 'quiet rage'.

The poet may have wanted us to think about the fact that Autumn is part of life, there are good times in life but they can be stolen away from us and make us feel empty and shaken just like the trees. A phrase I find interesting is 'an experienced robber' because the poet is comparing Autumn to a robber in a way that Autumn steals away the warm months and the colourful trees the way a robber would steal something that does not belong to him.

Strong opening – shows understanding of image straightaway.

Using selected detail well to show understanding.

Exploring subtext – personal response.

Understands imagery.

Examiner's comments

This extract from a response shows a clear grasp of the imagery and has an overview – an understanding of what the poem is about. This answer already has plenty of grade C qualities.

Your turn!

Read the poem on the following page carefully, jotting down notes and underlining key words and phrases as you do so; then complete the following task.

Write about the poem and its effect on you.

You may wish to include some or all of these points:

- the poem's content – what it is about
- the ideas the poet may have wanted us to think about
- the mood or atmosphere of the poem
- how it is written – words or phrases you find interesting, the way the poem is structured or organised, and so on
- your response to the poem.

Timing

Remember you only have 30 minutes in the exam! Take about 10 minutes for thinking and note-making before you start writing.

Tips

- Be sure to use the bullet points.
- Don't forget to use the title to help you understand what the poem is about.
- Select and highlight detail to support your overview (main point).

Woman Work

I've got the children to tend
The clothes to mend
The floor to mop
The food to shop
5 Then the chicken to fry
The baby to dry
I got company to feed
The garden to weed
I've got the shirts to press
10 The tots to dress
The cane to be cut
I gotta clean up this hut
Then see about the sick
And the cotton to pick,

15 Shine on me, sunshine
Rain on me, rain
Fall softly, dewdrops
And cool my brow again.

Storm, blow me from here
20 With your fiercest wind
Let me float across the sky
'Til I can rest again.

Fall softly, snowflakes
Cover me with white
25 Cold icy kisses and
Let me rest tonight.

Sun, rain, curving sky
Mountain, oceans, leaf and stone
Star shine, moon glow
30 You're all that I can call my own.

Maya Angelou

Appendix

GCSE English Literature – A quick guide to what the examiners are looking for at each grade

G	Very short responses, or with lots just copied out, with major parts missing or wrong.
F	General comments, with no real detail.
E	Focus on the question, with some selection of key parts of the text, but still not very developed.
D	More references to the text, with some discussion and awareness of characters, themes, mood and atmosphere and subtext (reading between the lines).
C	Detailed reference to the text – selecting and highlighting detail in a thorough, systematic, and purposeful way.
B	Really thorough and thoughtful discussion, with points well supported by evidence.
A	Analysis of how the text is written – unpicking the text to show how it works. Evaluation. Overview. Sensitivity.
A*	Doing all the A things consistently and well, with real confidence and succinctness.

Tips

- Detailed reference to the text is the key to getting a grade C or above. You need to know those set texts inside out, then use that knowledge to focus clearly on the questions asked.

- Although you need to show how the text works in order to achieve the higher grades, you do **not** need to 'spot' features. What is important is that you look at the words chosen and the way the texts are written; then you need to show your understanding of how these help to shape the writers' meanings.

- The higher the grade, the more focused and organised the response – so think for a minute or two before you write!